Expecting the Broken Brain to Do Mental Pushups

A Personal Journey to Understanding Schizophrenia and Depression

by Dave Elder

ISBN-10: 1479116904

ISBN-13: 978-1479116904

website: mentalpushups.com

This title is also available as an ebook.
See website for details.

Also, if you're interested in my other life
(as a musician) you can find out more at
daveelder.com.

*To the two women who gave me the story
and the reasons to write it,
my mother and the woman I call M
who has shared many good
and bad times with me.*

Table of Contents

Introduction

At the age of three and a half, my mother disappeared. The woman who took her place looked the same and had the same name, but was a very different person. When my mother came home after the birth of my younger brother, she had a broken brain. Everyone in the family knew something was wrong with Mom by the way she acted, but none of us came close to understanding it. At some point during my teenage years I learned the word *schizophrenia*, but knowing the word and its dictionary definition did not help me to better understand my mother. In fact, at the time it seemed to be a term without a clear meaning — it described something real, but that real thing did not have a clear shape. It was a shadowy ghost in the night, and every time I tried to reach out and touch it, it changed form, slipped from my grasp and faded into the darkness with a mocking laugh at my simple and vain attempt to understand.

For much of the next four decades, I saw a sad dynamic play out between my mother and the people who cared for her and looked after her, and I would imagine that something similar has happened and continues to happen in the homes of others who have the same or similar conditions. My father and the couple who had adopted my mother all treated her as if her mental problem was a choice she made. Many times I heard one of them threaten my mother by telling her that if she *went off the deep end* that they'd take her up to the State Hospital and she'd get shock treatments. The mention of the words *shock treatment* always brought a look of fear to Mom's eyes, and I understood that they were verbally and mentally spanking her for being a *bad* girl. She internalized this idea, and to the very end of her life, she would sometimes apologize for being a bad girl.

By the time I graduated high school and left home, I had given up trying to understand Mom. I accepted the fact that she was *crazy* in some very real sense, and when I would visit the family I would feel badly for all of them as the sad dynamic between them continued to play out, but I also felt I could do nothing to change it.

When I began dating a woman who I'll call M, I had no more understanding of the term *clinical depression* than I had of the word *schizophrenia*, but M spoke about her condition as if it was a broken arm, except that the broken arm was inside of her head, where no one could see it. During an episode of her illness which she went through as we began living together, I still had no grasp of the nature of the broken brain. Not long after she emerged from this episode, however, my father died, and I became much more closely involved in my mother's care than I had ever been, and over the next few years, I came to clearly see the real meaning of both schizophrenia and clinical depression (also know as major depression, unipolar depression, unipolar disorder, major depressive disorder and recurrent depressive disorder).

Imagine a man with a broken arm. Now imagine the family and friends of this person asking and expecting him to do pushups. The family and friends of the broken arm person keep telling him that if he tries hard enough, and believes strongly enough, he can do it. Try as he might, he'll never do those pushups, and he feels a lot of pain every time he tries. However, his family and friends grow impatient with him for not fulfilling their request, and they tell him he's not trying hard enough. They lose respect for him, and they chide him for not really wanting to succeed. They tell him he's a bad person with a serious character flaw. They tell him the problem is all in his head, and if he truly cared, he could fix it himself just by thinking about it. If he dares to complain about the pain, his family and friends call him a *cry baby*.

Who would treat a man with a broken arm so cruelly? Probably no one who could actually see the broken arm.

But what about the people with broken brains? So many of us who aren't trained psychologists or psychiatrists think we understand what's wrong with these people who have mental problems, and we can judge them and tell them how they ought to act to be better people. I often dismissed people with mental problems as *cry babies* who weren't willing to face up to the tough realities of life, when, given my own family history, I should have known better. However, when I found myself in a place where I really needed to understand, I finally saw that broken brain quite clearly, and having seen it, I think

My mother in the summer of 1958. I think this picture was taken at the Toledo Zoo. She was by now hearing voices in her head, though we often didn't know when.

I have a duty to pass on that understanding to as many of my fellow *normal* people as I can. In this book I hope to do just that by bringing the reader along on my journey, which began at my mother's bedside at the tender age of three and a half. I broke through to a much clearer understanding during one of M's major episodes of depression, but my journey to greater understanding continues to this day.

People often speak of mental conditions in mystic terms, and some say that maybe *crazy* people actually see things more clearly than the rest of us, or perhaps the people who hear voices are communicating with other dimensions and/or departed spirits. The reality of mental disease is that it's often actually just as mundane as a broken arm but harder to understand because it can't be seen as clearly. Modern forms of mental imaging continue to give us greater understanding of these problems, though, and we continue to refine our attempts to correct the chemical imbalances that some of our less fortunate friends and family members have gotten inside of the heads as a result of their genetic coding. I hope that with greater understanding will come greater compassion for those most in need of it, and better ways of caring for them.

Chapter 1

What Happened to Mom?

I made my first big mistake in life at the age of three and a half — I let my mother go. I knew at the time it was wrong, I knew I shouldn't let her go, but she and my grandmother both pleaded with me — they told me she had to go, but she would come back soon, and she would bring me a baby sister or brother with her when she came back.

I will admit that the idea of a little sister or brother sounded good. I'd already figured out that my older brother seemed to be missing a few cards in his deck, and I liked the idea of having a *normal* playmate. Still, I knew I shouldn't let my mother go. I sensed a danger in her leaving, that she might not come back. I knew I should hold her as tightly as I could until she changed her mind and stayed, but I didn't — I gave in to her and my grandmother. I let her go.

The days passed, and every day, every hour that she didn't return, I became more convinced that I'd been right. I'd made a big mistake, and I couldn't change it, I couldn't make it right. My mother didn't come back. I never should have let her go. I didn't feel guilty, though. While guilt would soon become a nearly constant companion of my childhood, this time I knew I hadn't caused whatever had happened to Mom. I had no guilt, but plenty of regret.

My father and grandmother brought my little brother home. I had hoped for a little sister, but a brother was OK. "Just let him be normal," I prayed silently, wordlessly. I quietly pleaded with God, or whatever spirit in the air might have an invisible hand in such matters. As a baby he looked normal enough, from what you could tell about a baby. I knew I couldn't really tell about him for a while, but I had hope.

Of course, I also had a big head start on him, at three and a half. I knew I'd have to be patient with him. My older brother had more than two years on me, but I felt as if in some ways I'd already caught up to him. I thought I could probably protect little brother from older brother's influence, and I would help him to grow up *normal* as much as I could help.

I don't remember my mother as a *normal* young woman. I remember her as my playmate, crawling along the dining room floor with me, and I missed her after she had gone. Grandma would play with me sometimes, but most of the time she had other things to do. I didn't see Dad and Grandpa much — most of the time they were only home in the evenings and usually not in the mood to play. Sometimes I would play with older brother, but soon he started going to school and wasn't around as much either, so I had to get used to playing solo.

One day not long after Dad brought little brother home, he took older brother and me to visit Mom, at the place she was now staying on Clinton Street in Binghamton. Dad parked the car and we walked up the sidewalk to a building that didn't look much like a hospital. I asked Dad about it, and he told me it wasn't a hospital, it was an outpatient clinic, but I had no idea what *that* was. When we walked in, I saw a lot of people in beds, but most of them didn't look that bad. No one was coughing or holding a thermometer in their mouth. I saw no bandages, casts, crutches, medical machines or any of the usual stuff that you would expect to see around sick people.

Then we came to my mother's bed. She was laying in bed, she smiled to see us and she hugged and kissed us all. Not knowing any better, I asked her why she didn't come home, and she smiled at me and said, "I've been sick." As she said it, she looked at me in a way that said, "You understand what I'm saying." If she had actually said that, I would have replied, "No, Mom, I don't understand." Laying there, she looked well enough. She did not look sickly in any way. What was wrong?

My mother as a *normal* young woman around Christmas in 1950, long before the real trouble began. Since I was born eight and a half months later, she was already pregnant with me, though she might not have known.

My father in the early 1950s as a dapper young man, albeit one who couldn't even support his wife and one child, let alone the two others that would arrive in the next few years.

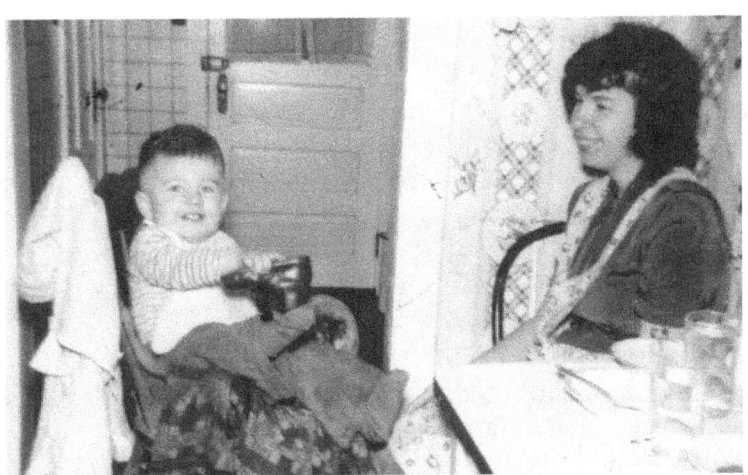

My mother and me. Judging from my size, I'd say this would have been well before my first birthday.

What did she have? Was it serious? From the way she and my father spoke, it seemed to be. Would she die? I didn't think so, because it didn't seem to be that kind of *serious*. I did understand at that point that whatever Mom's sickness was, I shouldn't ask too many questions about it, so I didn't.

Before we left, I *did* ask her a question, though. I said, "Are you coming home?" She said, "I can't." Once again, the tone of her answer seemed to imply that I understood why, which of course I didn't. Over 30 years later I would visit her in the psychiatric ward of a hospital, and when I walked out, we would look at each other in much the same way, and I would still not know why she couldn't come home. My journey to understanding had just begun on that spring day in 1955, and I had no idea how long that journey would take.

When we walked back to the car, we didn't say much. As good boys, older brother and I walked the way we felt we should walk — quietly, soberly, the way we walked into church on Sunday morning. When we got to the car, it had a flat tire, and my father, who was one of the kindest and most gentle

Mom on the right with the man who had raised her on the left, in a moment that seems like it might have been a bit heated. She had already disappointed the couple who had raised her by marrying a man who couldn't support her and her first child, but she would disappoint them on a whole new level after the birth of her third child.

Expecting the Broken Brain to Do Mental Pushups

souls to ever walk the earth, kicked that tire very hard. In all our time together, I rarely saw him lose his temper, though I often saw him frustrated by the things in life that were beyond his control. This time he couldn't help it. I didn't know at the time what my mother's sickness meant to his life as he looked into the future, and how it closed the door on his most important plans and dreams. I could tell, though, that when he kicked that tire, his anger came from something much bigger than the tire itself. He believed in a kind and loving God, and this almighty deity who had power to intervene in the lives of lowly human beings, and sometimes did, had dealt him a very cruel hand indeed. God had given him a third son, but in the bargain his wife had lost her mind.

Not long after Mom finally came home, a few months later, she was gone again. She and my father took a train ride to Erie, Pennsylvania, to visit friends. Everyone — Dad, Grandpa and Grandma — said it would be good for Mom's nerves. I began to hear a lot about my mother's nerves.

Old brother, me and Mom, ready for church on Sunday. From the looks I would guess Mom was pregnant with little brother when we posed for this picture.

I remember standing on the platform at the train station, saying good-bye to Mom and Dad. Older brother and I stood there waving, with Grandpa and Grandma standing by us, as Mom and Dad stood in the doorway of the final train car and waved at us as the train pulled away, slowly at first but going faster, until they were soon out of sight. How I wished I could go with them. I loved trains, and the idea of riding in a passenger car for miles and miles sounded so exciting. The destination — Erie, Pennsylvania — sounded so exotic, and a little spooky in a fun, *Halloween* kind of way. I would miss them while they were gone, but being home without them was all right. Grandpa and Grandma took care of everything pretty well, even if they didn't have much time to play.

As much as my parents' leaving had been an event, their return was not an event. No one told us that they were coming back. I remember them walking through the door with their suitcases. I was glad to see them, and I hugged them, but they quickly retreated to their room upstairs as if they were sneaking into some place where they didn't belong. An unspoken expectation about Mom's return had hung in the air, and now the reality spoke only of emptiness.

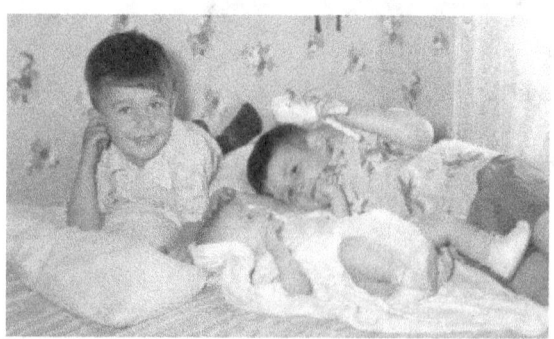

Me on the left with older brother. We both were obviously enjoying our new little playmate, younger brother.

What had we expected? I didn't quite know it at the time, though as I neared and passed my fourth birthday I came to understand as I became part of the household *we*. *We* the family, who would struggle to figure out what to do about Mom, had all hoped, without saying, that Mom would *really* return. Would the woman who left months earlier to give birth to little brother ever come back? Could that almighty and caring God work a small miracle for a family of humble, faithful followers? Was that too much to ask? Evidently it was, though at the time I didn't know how big a miracle that would have been.

So my mother's return in the flesh would disappoint everyone. All the effort and expense of sending her and my father to Erie for two weeks had not improved her nerves. As they arrived home, they quickly hurried to the upstairs room where she would often take refuge in the coming years, hiding not so much from me and my two brothers, but more from the couple who had raised her from the age of two. This couple had loved and cared for her, and she now felt she could do nothing to please them. Mom had come back, but she was now not the same woman who had left, and she never would or could be.

I'm in the chair holding little brother with older brother and Mom looking on. Mom was by now a very troubled young woman.

Older brother and me, in the summer of 1958. I believe we were at the Toledo Zoo when we posed for this one. Ironically, I didn't even know at the time what the words *rock 'n roll* meant. I just liked the look of the hat and somehow I managed to persuade the folks to buy it for me.

Older brother with my childhood buddy D. D would have been about 10 in this picture. His conflicts with his father were already a big part of his life, though we didn't know that. He didn't know then that he carried the same genetic curse as his father.

Chapter 2

D's Father and Shattered Nerves

I might have been ten, or maybe eleven. It was probably summer — a bright, sunny, long warm morning that my friend D from across the road and I could fill with whatever games we chose. Along the way, D said we should stop in and see his dad, who was painting the boat that day. D's parents had bought the place next door a few years earlier, renting out the house and the trailer behind the house while using the barn for storage and a work space. Among other things, they were storing their most prized possession, their boat, in the barn.

The boat was a wonder to me. I knew my own parents and grandparents could never own a boat, but if my good friend's parents had a boat, it was still a likely possibility that I could get to ride on it someday. Sometimes in those years such thoughts could make me feel as if the future held unlimited possibilities. Someday I would ride that boat, with my friend D and his family — all good people I liked pretty well — and maybe we'd eat hamburgers and drink sodas and enjoy the feeling of riding on the water. Maybe we'd swim. Well, probably I wouldn't, since I still couldn't swim, but maybe I'd get to see D's older sister in a swimsuit.

I remember that when we went into the barn, D's dad was working with a trouble light, a paint can and a paint brush. I remember that he dropped the brush, and D had to help him pick it up. D's father seemed a bit agitated, for no apparent reason, and that seemed to make D a bit jumpy. I could not have guessed at the waves of emotion breaking inside of both of them — waves that they kept just below the surface, just beyond my view.

Later I asked D about his father, and he told me a story good enough to satisfy my curiosity and explain the strange behavior. Probably his parents had invented the tale, and though it didn't quite add up, I believed it. He told me that his father's nerves had been shattered by a recent car accident. I hadn't known about the accident, when it supposedly happened, but as a kid I didn't really keep a close watch on other peoples' lives.

A few weeks later, talking with D, I mentioned the car accident, and he didn't seem to know what I meant. When I repeated the bit about his father being in a car accident that had shattered his nerves, D told me that I was confused, and that the accident happened to someone else. *That* someone else was, according to D, another adult male we both knew, though I've long since forgotten who it was. Having known D as a playmate for many years, I knew very well that sometimes he didn't tell the truth. In fact, once in a while he would lie just to see if he could make me believe something. In this case, I simply ended up being confused. I didn't know what the real story was concerning his father, and maybe that was what D really wanted.

Over the next couple of years, whenever I spent time with D's family, I looked more carefully at his father, but I didn't observe anything of particular significance. D's father didn't seem to have any lasting physical problems, if a car accident had occurred. He seemed to have the full use of his hands, his arms, his legs, and his neck, and I didn't see any wounds of any kind. D's father did seem to act more agitated more often, but I couldn't say whether he had changed in that regard, or if I simply noticed it more since I started paying more attention.

I wondered about the idea of a person with shattered nerves. Supposedly, my mother's nerves had been shattered by the birth of little brother, but what did that mean? When a glass shattered, only pieces remained, and those pieces could not go back together. I figured out that when a person had shattered nerves, the nerves actually didn't shatter — they were all still there, and all still working, but was there some difference inside of them? When I got to ninth grade biology class, I thought maybe I'd find an answer, but as so often was the case, my schoolwork, while opening my eyes to greater understanding of other aspects of life, didn't connect to my own burning personal mysteries.

People is this time often used terms like *high strung* and *too sensitive* when referring to someone with mental problems, and I often heard my mother spoken of this way. These terms seemed to imply that someone's nerves could be wound too tightly, as if nerves were strings on a guitar or a violin. Anyone who plays one of these instruments can tell you that if you try

From right to left, that's me, younger brother, my friend D, older brother and D's twin sister, all waiting for the school bus in 1961. As is usual with the condition that killed D's father, D carried the disease but his twin sister did not. Of his two other siblings, his older sister carried the disease as well and his older brother did not.

to turn a string much higher than its designated pitch, that string will break. Somehow, a person with mental problems had nerves wound too tightly, and those nerves broke, in some mysterious way. The break wasn't physical — the person could still feel hot and cold or a pin prick on the end of any one of those nerves, but inside the person, the nervous system was somehow broken, although somehow still physically intact.

Why did a person have a nineteenth nervous breakdown? Nerves, like wires, carry electric pulses, but when you overload a wire, it burns. Did a person have a nervous breakdown because their nerves got overloaded? If so, how did that happen? The nerves didn't burn out from the overload, but somehow the overload caused a major problem with the main central processing unit, called *the brain*. Why, and how? Could you prevent the overload if you kept the current down in the nerves? If you kept a person tranquil, perhaps with a tranquilizer, could that prevent the overload? If you kept a person from feeling anything too intensely, such as anger or sadness, could you keep that person from a nervous breakdown?

During the time I grew up, and for some years afterwards, my mother regularly took a prescription sedative, to keep her basically calm. This did not prevent her from occasionally *going off the deep end* but we the family believed it helped to keep her on a steady course day to day without major problems. During much of his childhood and well into his adulthood, older brother took a reduced dosage of the same sedative, interestingly enough. It did occur to me as well that possibly D's father might benefit from such a prescription, although he might have had one and I simply didn't know about it.

Around the time I headed for that ninth grade biology class for the first time, my buddy D and his family moved to another part of town, only a few miles away, but far enough to effectively end our close friendship. He would no longer show up at the back door and ask if I could come out to play. Since he was two years behind me in school, I wouldn't even see him around the high school campus until I hit junior year, and by then we had almost become strangers. I think his father died during my senior year, and I have a vague memory of writing a sympathy card to D, following my grandmother's instruction to do so.

D's father was not much older than my father, and so he seemed to have died at a relatively young age, although from the talk I heard, the death seemed to have followed some inevitable course. People spoke in vague terms about how his health had severely declined in the final years, and once again I heard intimations about some auto accident but got no specifics about where, when or how.

I moved on with my life, and not long after that I began my freshman year at Northwestern University in Evanston, Illinois, about 800 miles from the old home town. While there a couple of years later, I spoke with little brother on the phone, and he told me he'd recently seen D around town. Little brother was still in high school at the time, but D had graduated. From little brother's description D sounded pretty much like a young adult version of the kid who had been my childhood friend. The kid I knew had a lot of energy, and also a taste for danger much greater than my own. For example, it wasn't enough to ride a bike down Ross Hill Road, the steepest hill in the neighborhood — D had to try it with his feet off the pedals. When he wanted to set up a bicycle jump in my back yard, he told my grandfather that we were daredevils. I had no desire to be such a daredevil, but I usually went along with whatever crazy idea he came up with, hoping that it wouldn't involve too much pain.

So from little brother's description of D, it sounded like he made it to young adulthood all right, despite the death of his father at a somewhat younger age. However, something changed very soon afterwards, and I didn't know exactly what that was. I would occasionally visit the home town during the 1970s, and I spoke with D's mother while she worked her job at a local grocery store. She told me that D felt so discouraged about life that he didn't want to do anything. D didn't want to go out, look for a job, meet girls, go to a bar, ride a bike, drive a car — he had no desire to do anything. I couldn't understand it — what had happened to him? Each time she told me this, she said it as if I understood some untold part of the story. In fact, it reminded me of the tone my mother used in the bed at the psychiatric center when I was three and a half and she said, "I'm sick." Once again, I seemed to lack a key bit of information that someone assumed I understood, and I didn't quite know how to ask the question, because I didn't know what question to ask.

I decided that if I ever met D himself, I would say to him, "What's wrong with you? Why can't you just get over this? What's your problem?" I thought I could give him a verbal kick in the pants and help him get through whatever had tangled his wires. Fortunately for us both, I didn't run into him on the street, and I didn't put the effort into actually tracking him down. By the time we finally met again, I would know what his problem was.

Chapter 3

Mom's Real Parents

A short drive from my childhood home, about an hour away, lies the little upstate town of Freeville. Growing up, I didn't know that town's history, or how it got its name, but I knew the roads that led to it, and I didn't like going there. I enjoyed the ride, and the beautiful country we travelled through, but going to Freeville meant one thing — visiting Mom's real mother.

The couple who owned the home I grew up in, and who I called my grandfather and grandmother, had adopted my mother. I didn't know the story during my childhood years, but my mother's real mother had *gone off the deep end* following the birth of my mother's younger brother. What I did know then was that my mother's real mother was a crazy old lady who lived in this funky little house just outside of Freeville. I didn't exactly love using the outhouse there, but I could deal with that — after all, we had a few other relatives and friends with the old style outdoor facilities. For example, the parents of the grandmother we lived with were an older couple who lived in a house up on a hill in Apalachin that had no electricity or running water.

I had a very simple reason for not wanting to visit Mom's real mother. As my father said on more than one occasion, the smell in that little house would *knock you over*. Mom's real mother had at least a dozen cats, and another five or six dogs. I'm not sure if the woman actually knew the exact number of dogs and cats, but the total was certainly four or five times what she should have had in her little place.

More than once, Dad, younger brother and I would hang around outside, even on the cold weather days. We would sit in the car, and hold out as long as we could. In the struggle between the increasing cold and the smell, if the visit went on long enough, and it usually did, we would end up having to go inside to warm up when we couldn't stand the cold any longer.

On one visit, my father mentioned that when the old lady died, if she willed the house to him and my mother, he would donate the place to the local fire department and let them use the place for practice. He had no desire to try to salvage anything useful from inside that little house. At the time we would never have guessed that Mom's real mother, a good twenty years older than my father, would outlive him and actually live to see the new millennium while he did not.

My mother would remain devoted to her birth mother for as long as the woman lived. As a child I did not know that my mother's real mother had, like Mom, become a schizophrenic following the birth of her third child, and that she had also spent time at the State Hospital in Binghamton. Family members would hint at parts of the story, and seemed to assume that I knew the rest.

My mother would also curse her own real father to the end of her days. As much as she loved her own mother, she hated her own father, and seemed to blame him for what had happened to her mother. Some form of this basic notion seemed to float around other family members though it was never clearly stated or given exact meaning. Mom's real father had divorced her real mother after the schizophrenia emerged, and divorce, at that time, was looked upon by religious families such as ours as being a cardinal sin worthy of eternal damnation. Beneath the surface of the facts, some idea of infidelity lurked. Had Mom's real father cheated on his wife before the divorce? Did he have another woman, or more, on the side, earlier in the marriage? Did he somehow force Mom's real mother *off the deep end* so he could get a divorce from her and go start another family with another woman? After all, he did remarry and have other children. How much of what happened to Mom's real mother was caused by her real father? It remained an open and unanswered question for a long time, but whatever the real answer, my mother had come to her own conclusion, and she would forever hold him responsible.

By the time I reached high school, I had already seen at least one or two old movies in which a woman was committed to an asylum even though she wasn't really *crazy*. The plot involved either a cheating husband who wanted to change wives or a criminal villain who needed to keep this woman quiet because she actually knew details that could possibly tie him to his crimes. If such a plot could make a believable movie story line, could it also explain what happened to Mom's real mother?

The house my mother's real mother lived in when I was growing up looked like this in 2004, a couple of decades after the old woman had moved out. She lived with her oldest daughter's family for a number of years but spent the last years of her life in a nursing home.

We, the three boys, thought little about the matter, and we would only meet Mom's real father once. It happened during the fairer weather months of 1968, when he came to our home for a brief visit. My two brothers tell me I was there, but apparently at the time I had so little interest in him, or even curiosity about him, that I don't even clearly remember the meeting. He had moved to the Chicago area, where he lived and worked as a detective. In less than two years, I would be living in that area, going to college in Evanston, Illinois, but not once during the almost nine years I lived there did it ever occur to me to try to contact him. I didn't despise the man as my mother did, but I didn't see any compelling reason to try to connect with him.

Chapter 4

A Trip to the State Hospital

I don't remember the year, but it happened some time during my high school years, and it would probably have been somewhere between 1966 and 1968. It was an early Saturday evening, some time during the school year, not close to any memorable holiday or occasion. I remember the weather as being cool but not really cold — it could have been mid-April or mid-October. I don't remember what I was doing, and whether I was involved with school work, reading for pleasure or playing my guitar. What I do remember was that my grandmother interrupted my activity, whatever it was, to tell me Dad needed my help. Grandma didn't give me any details, she just asked me to come up to the parent's room upstairs.

When I came to their bedroom, I quickly understood the need for my help. Mom sat in a chair, with a strange smile on her face and her hands next to her ears, snapping her fingers. It looked like Mom was starting into one of her episodes, and Dad would have to take her to the State Hospital in Binghamton. As Mom's favorite child, my role would be to help him persuade her to go. During a schizophrenic episode, she would trust the word of her favorite son more than the word of her husband.

It took some time, but we finally persuaded Mom to walk down and get into the car with us. Instead of taking the Vestal Parkway, we drove along Main Street from Endicott through Johnson City and Binghamton. I think my father drove down Main Street so that if Mom made any sudden strange moves, he could pull over to the curb. Also, it may have made Mom feel better going slower along a regular street.

It was already a late hour, with very little traffic on the street, and I remember that of the dozens of traffic lights we went through, we got the green light at almost all of them, waiting for only two or three red lights on the way. At the time I thought that seemed a bit odd, though I also thought that perhaps some mechanical reason might account for our green light good fortune.

I don't remember phone calls, but someone must have made one or two, because on our arrival at the State Hospital in Binghamton, we soon found ourselves in an office with Mom's psychiatrist. I listened as he asked her question about the voices she was hearing. This may have been the moment when I understood Mom's official diagnosis — I remember hearing the term *schizophrenia* and knew that it was meant to describe Mom's behavior. Mom was hearing voices, and she had snapped her fingers next to her ears to try to not hear those voices.

As I listened to her psychiatrist ask questions, I wondered how much he really did understand her. Maybe he didn't understand at all. What if schizophrenia was a slippery term trying to define an indefinable ghost in the dark? I didn't know what he knew, or even what was knowable. What Dad and I understood then, though, was that he and I could do nothing for her. She agreed, under urging from her psychiatrist, to stay in the hospital for a while, for an unspecified period of time, during which she could get a better handle on dealing with those voices she heard.

Dad and I left her there at the State Hospital, and drove home. We said almost nothing. I knew my father felt discouraged and sad, and I couldn't say anything that would make him feel better. I also felt a great sense of emptiness. I could do nothing for Mom, and I couldn't understand her. At that moment, and for much of the next few years, I felt very distant from my mother. I became aware then of my lack of feeling for my own mother, and that lack of feeling would sometimes trouble me in a vague sort of way, but I had plenty to do to keep me busy, and I tried not to think about it very much.

My father and I got home around daylight on Sunday morning. Before we could go to bed, we had to deliver the newspapers for my route. Actually, I had to deliver them — he didn't have to help out, but he or my grandfather almost always did, and this morning he did it with me as he usually did. I think we both got to bed around 8 a.m. We rarely if ever missed church on Sunday morning, but this time we didn't go, and we had no guilt. I think Dad felt, as I did, that due to the circumstances God would not frown on us because of our absence.

This is what the State Hospital in Binghamton looked like in 2012. The main building is no longer in use.

Chapter 5

The Strip in Atlanta

I got my first glimpse of Atlanta, Georgia, from an airplane window, flying in from Chicago, on June 10, 1971, and I liked what I saw. Instead of a vast sea of grey concrete below me, as I had seen leaving Chicago, Atlanta looked very green from up there, and from that first impression I thought I would really like it when I got down to the ground.

Atlanta did not disappoint me when I got down to ground level that day. I found myself walking block by block through the greenest urban setting I had ever encountered at that point in my life. While it had plenty of the required freeways and tall buildings, Atlanta also had lots of tree-lined streets and spacious green parks.

I would find much to like about Atlanta over that summer, but walking the final block to my destination, I saw something not so attractive. As an introduction to what my Atlanta summer would show me, I saw a guy nodding out in an alley. I had never seen someone nodding out before, but somehow I knew that this fellow wasn't simply drunk or sleepy.

Growing up in a semi-rural upstate New York town in the 1960s, I knew about the exploding drug scene in a very distant way. In Vestal we had all of the great 1960s music, but the drug scene, like the anti-war protests, happened somewhere else, even though Bethel was actually less than a hundred miles away. Going to college in the Chicago area, I had become aware of how easily I could have purchased marijuana or LSD from campus connections if so inclined, but I didn't have any interest in spending what little cash I had on either of those. Hard drugs like heroin or cocaine didn't make the campus scene much at the time, though — they weren't cool, mind-expanding substances.

When I first became aware of heroin, opium and cocaine, they seemed like stronger, much more evil versions of *demon rum*. I grew up in a very religious household with parents and grandparents who never touched alcohol. I had my first taste of something alcoholic in Europe the summer after my high school graduation, and even then it happened by mistake — I hadn't quite understood the translation, and I thought I was getting a glass of grape juice. As a young adult a long distance from my parents' home, I had decided that alcohol wasn't the evil substance my religious family felt it was, but I also didn't have any great interest in it.

Over the previous months prior to my summer in Atlanta, the Southern Baptist group I associated with at Northwestern had opened up a Christian outreach center in an area near the Chicago and Evanston border, on the Chicago side. The center pulled in a group of alcoholics who lived on the nearby streets, and managed to convert a couple of them to the Southern Baptist faith. I noticed pretty quickly, though, that the conversions didn't last long. An alcoholic would *find Jesus*, and then make an effort to try a new lifestyle, but it all fell apart pretty quickly. The group would provide a setting where the guy could *clean up* — he could shave and shower on a daily basis, he was given better clothes to wear, and he was given the chance to try to begin a new life, but within a week or two the guy would disappear and end up back on the street, begging for quarters to buy his next pint. The only conclusion I could draw at the time was that the alcoholics would rather live on the street and beg for money to buy booze than make the effort to try for a better life, and apparently even a new-found faith in Jesus couldn't change their outlook. I couldn't understand why someone would make that choice, but I also didn't think I needed to get too involved in other people's lives.

So by the summer of 1971, as a 19-year-old, I had concluded that alcoholics and heroin addicts were all losers, though the heroin addicts were definitely worse. I had no particular interest in any substance abuse, and I didn't understand the attraction. I had seen a few alcoholics, and I didn't know why anyone would want to follow their example. I had never seen any junkies before, but nothing I had read about heroin made it sound interesting. Seeing the guy nodding out in the alleyway, I thought *that* didn't look like something I wanted to do.

During the previous year I had also seen Laura Nyro onstage in Chicago, and I felt the most powerful song she performed that night was a tune called *Been on a Train*. She made no mention of heroin in the lyrics, but even someone like me who didn't always catch the slang terms and street references to the drug scene could clearly understand the nature of the story in this song. The junkie in the song dies, as street junkies often do, and from the way Ms. Nyro performed the tune that night, it felt very much like a true story, and one that had left her with a very deep and painful memory. I had no personal attraction to living dangerously, and couldn't imagine any sort of feeling a drug could give me that would make me feel like risking my life for it.

I finally arrived at my destination, on the block between Tenth Street and Eleventh on Peachtree Street NE. In the middle of that block, on the east side of the street, in the center of a six-block area called *The Strip* which had become the core of Atlanta's counterculture community, a Christian minister had established a *hippie outreach center* designed to lure young freaks away from the drug lifestyle and into the Southern Baptist Church. Having moved my religious affiliation in the Evanston area to the SBC due to a lack of a nearby GARBC (northern Baptist) group, I had signed on as a summer missionary to work at the Aurora.

While that minister would say, with some obvious dissatisfaction, when we met again the following year, "It looks like we turned you into a hippie," I was already one when I arrived, and I didn't consider *Christian* and *hippie* to be mutually exclusive terms. That summer, I and a few fellow Jesus freaks often made the case for Jesus being the original hippie. I saw my role at the Aurora as being a sort of spiritual lifeguard. If someone was drowning in the drug lifestyle, and they felt they needed spiritual help, I could give them guidance. I didn't feel particularly obligated to bring anyone into the SBC fold, and as the summer progressed I felt less and less connected to any organized church. I could show someone how to find Jesus, and I was happy to do so, especially if it might help someone overcome a drug problem, but I didn't think steering them toward the SBC would necessarily benefit them. I truly believed that the personal spiritual experience mattered most, and could offer the most to someone trying to find their own footing. I had no concern for the minister's desire to increase the SBC membership.

So at the Aurora I wasn't a straight guy disguised as a hippie trying to reel in other hippies, get them off drugs and have them cut their hair, put on more acceptable clothes and join the SBC. I was all for the *getting off drugs* part, but that was the only part of *setting someone straight* that interested me. I believed in the counterculture that had blossomed from Haight-Ashbury to Bethel, and I felt completely at home on The Strip, even if the drug sellers on the street did sometimes annoy me a bit.

As an employee at the Aurora, I did have a few jobs to do. If I worked the closing shift, I'd have to collect the beer cans, and before too long I got very good at using a toilet plunger, since I found myself doing that at least once or twice every day. However, most of the time, I simply had to be there, hang out and mingle with the street people. In this era before the time clocks hit the street chess scene, I played a lot of the game, and met a few very good players who helped me sharpen my technique by beating me handily every time I made even one small mistake.

In this process, I met a lot of people around my age (nineteen) who had already developed serious drug dependencies. I tried to offer them advice when asked, and I did my best to act as a positive role model, but I had little understanding of their problems. I thought some might have adopted a drug lifestyle simply because they had no alternatives — they didn't want to follow the straight lifestyle, which seemed to offer nothing but crushing boredom and meaningless labor, but they couldn't think of any other path to follow. I personally felt no need to even experiment with drugs of any style. I had already found the core of my own personality in the role of singer/songwriter, and while I didn't know how to make the connection to the big time that the musicians I admired had done, I thought I would figure that puzzle piece out in my near future.

I felt that I had finally found my own musical identity just as the singer/songwriter era arrived. As a younger teenager, I had imitated the music I loved, from the Monkees to the Association to the Doors. I came up with original ideas for the words and music of my songs, but I borrowed the styles of other artists — one song would sound very much like a Beatles tune, another like a Doors song, another like a Box Tops track. The singer/songwriter era arrived just as I became an adult and felt the need to do some *serious* songwriting, moving beyond the little pop *ditties* that I had crafted as a child. I soaked up the influence of a whole batch of people just coming to the surface, like James Taylor, Cat Stevens, Laura Nyro and Neil Young, while also trying to pick up on as much as possible of the back catalogs and current albums of Bob Dylan, Judy Collins, Gordon Lightfoot, Arlo Guthrie, Joni Mitchell,

Leonard Cohen, Tom Rush and a few others. I had decided to quit looking for the band mates I never found, and going forward I would plan to simply write and perform as a solo act.

While tuning into a lot of *folkies* at the time, though, I also listened to the best of the current *classic* rock and the music that I had missed out on or had only caught the edges of in the previous few years. Shortly after Jimi Hendrix's death in September of 1970, I began spinning his albums regularly on my turntable. One song that caught my attention was, of course, *Manic Depression*. In the rock-and-roll tradition of exaggeration, I thought Jimi was going over the top a bit, and I didn't think he'd actually been through manic depression, though now looking back I'm not so sure. I had read briefly about manic depression in high school, but my impression at the time was that the description could apply to a lot of people, including myself. As a typical teenager, I was at the center of my own world, and a legend in my own mind, so I could picture myself saying the kind of things that manic types would. I also often felt sad enough that I could picture myself in the position of someone at the depression end of the circle, making a lot more out of my problems than what they really were. At that young age, I judged manic depression to be just a slightly sharper version of what *normal* people like myself often feel. A few years later, listening to Jimi Hendrix, I thought it likely that manic depression was a bit more serious condition that I had judged it to be in high school, though I didn't have a clear idea about it. As a college kid I was discovering that life had a lot more complexity than I had realized in high school.

I had worked at the Aurora for two or three weeks when a guy walked up to the door where I was standing at the time and asked if I knew where he could find musicians in the area. I told him he had come to exactly the right place, he had just met one, and all he had to do to meet more was to hang around. So he did.

Not long after that first meeting, we talked about songwriting. From the conversations he seemed to have a much different approach from my own. I spoke of songwriting in somewhat mystical terms, as part of a process of self-discovery. He spoke about it as a purely mechanical process, not much different from replacing spark plugs on a car. I concluded from the conversation that he probably wasn't that good. I had met a few people over the previous two years who called themselves songwriters, and each time I ended up disappointed when I heard the tunes. None of them wrote the kind of songs that captured my imagination the way that Gordon Lightfoot's songs or Tom Rush's recordings did.

Then the Aurora ran a little open mic segment. As I did my tune, I could sense my new friend picking up on it. Then he got up and did his song. I only heard him do that song once, but to this day I still remember the melody very clearly, and some of the lyrics. I don't even remember his name, but I remember his song's title, and listening to the song, I thought, "Hey, this guy is really good!"

Our friendship quickly developed into a budding musical partnership. We each wrote songs, sang, and played both guitar and piano, so we now had the core of a new super-group. All we needed was a bass player and a drummer, and he and I could supply the rest, with a lot a variety. We could both play guitar on a song, or we could each play a different keyboard such as a piano and organ combination, or one of us could play guitar and the other could do the keyboard, all while singing two-part harmony. For just two musicians, we could create a lot of different combinations together, and our singing and songwriting styles were highly complimentary. As a musical team of two young guys who had just met each other, we fit together very well, and we saw ourselves as a new Stills and Young team with a very bright future ahead of us.

Not long after our meeting, a drummer showed up at the Aurora looking for other musicians. I set up a rehearsal with him and my partner after hours at the place, and that night we all sounded very good together. The drummer had a bass player partner who couldn't make the rehearsal that night, but who could be there the next time around. The group was coming together, and it began to feel like the hand of destiny moving us all towards the ultimate stardom that awaited us not too far down the road.

One small snag in the dream appeared that night, though. A stranger came knocking on the glass front door, and my partner went over to speak with him. He said he was looking for drugs, and my partner told him he could sell him some heroin. Fortunately, the stranger didn't want heroin, and he walked away. I then had to tell my partner to cool it with trying to sell drugs in the place. I told him he could do whatever he wanted out on the street, but he couldn't deal drugs in the Aurora. Of the few responsibilities I had at the place, probably the most important was to keep dealers from selling drugs there, and here my partner had been trying to do just that. He accepted my scolding and agreed not to do *that* again, but I found his interest in heroin troubling, to say the least.

A few days later we met at a nearby park on my off time. With no particular plans, we hung out, checked out *the chicks* and played some guitar. Then we decided to play that old favorite musician dreamer game, *What are you going to do with your money when you get rich and famous?* I told him I wanted to buy a big place out in the country, probably an old farm with lots of land, in some place really nice, like maybe Vermont, and have the barn all set up as a rehearsal and recording studio, with a nice and big old farmhouse to live in. As I let my last words about the farm house hang, he added, "Yeah, with a big basement full of morphine." I said nothing to that, but in my head, I thought, "No, that's not what I had in mind."

Why morphine? Why heroin? Why would you need, or want, something like that? It seemed to me like a heavy, dark cloud settling over my sunny country idyllic vision. I had no interest in that, and I didn't begin to understand his.

A few days later came our next rehearsal, but this time, no drummer or bass player came. We didn't let that bother us too much, though. We knew we had the talent together to go somewhere, and finding a rhythm section would surely happen somehow, some way. We played new songs, we swapped musical ideas, and we admired each other's abilities. I began to realize just how good a guitar player he was, and as I stretched out a bit more on the piano than I had in the past, he told me how much he liked what he heard. We, the dynamic duo, were still on track as the future Next Big Thing, and we knew that we'd find a bass player and drummer in due time.

Our next rehearsal, though, was completely different — he didn't come. I hadn't known exactly where he lived, and I hadn't known his last name. I had no telephone number for him, or any contact information of any kind. As far as I know, he never walked into the Aurora again. Just that quickly, the future Next Big Thing ended. I never saw him again, and in a short time, I realized that I had even forgotten his name, though I never forgot him or that first song I heard him do. I thought that perhaps it was for the best, given his interest in heroin. Maybe I was better off not trying to be in a band with someone doing heroin, especially given all the possible legal consequences of such behavior.

Of course, I also had to wonder about what happened to him. I did think he might have ended up in jail, but that was almost a best-case scenario. I knew the way many junkies ended up, and I had a hunch that he may have met his end in some small, sparsely furnished room, shortly after putting a needle into his arm.

Being in the middle of the Atlanta drug culture that summer, I learned things I might not have known otherwise. I found out that Atlanta was a main stop on the heroin pipeline from Miami to New York City. Another thing I learned was that Atlanta dealers would sometimes cut their dope with other dangerous powders — there was even a rumor about rat poison being used — so there were other ways for junkies to die besides a simple overdose.

I went on with my life that summer, and I met a few other musicians at the Aurora, but no one like my former partner. At one Aurora open mic, I found out that a guy called Stony, who I had played a number of chess matches with, was also a talented country songwriter with a rich country baritone voice. I can still remember the chorus of one of his songs, and once in a while these days I'll put one of those lines into Google to see what comes up. So far nothing comes up, though I haven't given up trying, but I also don't expect much. I didn't know Stony very well, but I can guess at how he probably got his nickname, and that guess leads me to the thought that quite possibly he also may have died young.

I left Atlanta at the end of the summer in 1971, hitching up I-85 for a planned visit to my family in upstate New York. After that visit, I would head back to the concrete grey and brutal cold of the Chicago area, but as much as I disliked Chicago, I liked Atlanta, and I decided that I would one day return to that green jewel of the South.

Chapter 6

Cab Story

I began my short-lived career as a taxi driver in the late spring of 1973, driving for the Evanston Cab Company. I could walk the few blocks from my apartment to the job in less than ten minutes, and I could often spend my time in the car reading while sitting at the taxi stand waiting for a fare. It was not a good job, but for someone coming out of school without much work experience, it would do until I figured out my next move.

I soon learned that the *real money* to be made driving a cab, if such a phrase meant anything at all, had to be earned on the south side of Howard Street, driving in Chicago. At some point, in the middle of the summer, I decided to give that a try. I found out I would have to drive the night shift, 6 p.m. to 6 a.m., to get my foot in the car door, and I'd probably have to do that for at least 6 months to a year before getting a shot at the day shift.

I did at least one complete week, and it might have been two, but that was about all I could handle, driving a cab twelve hours at night and trying to sleep through the middle of hot Chicago-area summer days. I rarely saw my wife, even when she worked on the late shift at the restaurant. Also, the night crew faced a much greater potential threat from thieves with guns, which was a rare occurrence on the Evanston side of Howard Street.

In that short time, however, I had at least two fares memorable enough that some four decades later I haven't forgotten them. As I drove south on North Western Avenue around 1 a.m. on one of those nights, a pedestrian flagged me down from the curb. At first I felt I'd gotten really lucky, snagging a paying ride in that neighborhood at that hour.

When he got in the cab, I did what a cab driver always does — I asked him where he wanted to go. He gestured straight ahead and said, "It's on down here a ways." Having already driven a cab for a while in Evanston, I had picked up and delivered more than one fare that didn't know the address of their destination, so I started the meter and headed further south on North Western Avenue.

I quickly noticed something unique about this particular rider. He started off talking about how death would be discontinued within a few years, because "they weren't going to allow it any more." The crazy conversation, however strange, didn't necessarily make this rider that much different from another, although usually such strange talk was fueled by alcohol and/or other chemicals, and usually that fuel showed other tell-tale signs, but this rider did not look, sound or act drunk or high. I quickly realized that what *really* set this rider apart, however, was that my response, or lack of one, didn't make any difference to this fellow.

Part of the art of driving a taxi, and making money doing so, lies in quickly assessing what the customer wants, and since the size of a cabbie's tip may vary according to how well he or she understands this, cab drivers quickly learn how to make the customer feel comfortable. Does the rider want the driver to simply listen to him or her? Quite often. Does the rider want the driver to agree with him or her that an older brother got too big a share of the father's estate, or that the results of the recent election don't seem quite right? Sometimes. Does the rider want to actually engage the driver in conversation? Once in a while. Does the rider want the driver to simply get to the destination as soon as possible, with little or no conversation necessary? Now and then. But this rider was truly different. He wanted to talk, and he assumed I was listening, but he didn't seem to care about how, or even if, I responded at all. He was like a TV newscaster, telling a compelling story, or at least one he thought was so, and assuming that I, his audience, had to be listening, which of course I was, since I couldn't change the channel, though I was also having some problems trying to follow the story.

Every now and then I would have to interrupt him to ask for further directions, and we didn't seem to be getting any closer to his destination. We went a number of blocks in one direction, then we'd turn and go a few blocks in another direction, and then turn again, heading in the completely opposite direction from our heading two turns before. By this strange, round-about fashion, however, we did finally arrive at the place he appeared to want to go, and I pulled in through the gates, which were still open at 2 a.m., roughly an hour after I had picked him up. While I didn't recognize the place, I could tell immediately that it was some sort of mental institution, as it reminded me very much of the New York State Hospital in Binghamton where my mother, and her mother, had both spent time.

Pulling through the gates, I suddenly realized the basic nature of the character I had been driving around for about an hour — my passenger was *crazy* in some way. For all that I have come to understand about certain mental conditions in the decades since that night, I do not have any additional insight into that passenger's psychiatric state. I did understand that we had arrived at the place where he felt at home, but at that early hour of the morning, he didn't seem to know what to do, and of course, neither did I. I drove him around the grounds, and stopped in a few places when he asked. Twice he got out of the car and wandered around nearby, and then returned to the car. There was no one around, and all the buildings seemed to be locked up tight, with few if any lights showing. Finally, not knowing what to do, I drove back out through the gates.

I dropped my passenger a few blocks away from those gates. He didn't have any other destination, so it seemed like the best thing to do. I hoped, and I expected, that he would spend the night in that area, and walk back through the gates in the morning. At that time, I didn't know what else to do. I didn't ask him for any money — having figured out that he was a mental patient, I didn't think he even understood the idea of paying for a taxi ride.

With the benefit of 20/20 hindsight, I can now see that I could have, and should have, tried harder to connect my passenger with someone who could help him. Like so many other moments in my life, I realized some time afterwards how I might have handled the situation better, but I hope that it worked out all right for that strange passenger, though I'll probably never know if it did.

Chapter 7

Sylvia Plath
and the 1970s Junkie Parade

By early 1974, my wife and I had fled the frigid Chicago winter for the milder temperatures of Atlanta, Georgia. Some time in that late spring, K discovered *The Bell Jar* and read it cover to cover. We had often spoken about our *crazy* families and their many *strange* members. Around the time of our wedding a couple of years earlier, my new father-in-law pulled his daughter aside after meeting my family and asked her, "Is there something wrong with Dave's brothers?" I knew, even then, that my older brother had an official diagnosis, but I didn't know what it was. I had hoped that my younger brother, then in his final year of high school, had simply been twisted by the strange home circle, and that once he graduated and headed out into the world beyond that circle, he'd turn out all right.

At this point, however, I didn't think much about my family at all. I knew my mother was literally crazy, and maybe my older brother might be as well. During my college years, I had gotten used to saying, "My family is crazy," a phrase well known to all of my friends, being said by almost everyone at the time. I used to think, however, when I heard a friend say this, that probably he or she didn't have a mother who was a diagnosed schizophrenic, though today I do wonder if maybe some of them did. I have recently concluded that psychiatric problems may likely be more widespread among the human population than is currently recognized by the majority of people, but back in the early 1970s people were just beginning to acknowledge the mental problems of family members.

So when K started reading *The Bell Jar* I had no interest in it. The writer, Ms. Plath, did lose her father at a young age, and I could sympathize with her for that, but I also felt that everyone's life had challenges, and the key to living life was to rise to those challenges instead of being knocked over by them. I wanted to read about people who had overcome difficulty and learn from them. I didn't think I would find anything to learn from someone who had buckled when the tough times came along.

K read a few parts of the book to me that she thought were significant, and I listened, but I could find no sympathy for someone haunted by dark moods. I had plenty of moods myself, among them lots of anger and sadness, but I never felt myself lost inside of one, and I didn't see why I should care about someone who did have such utter lack of control. I also concluded that in some ways Ms. Plath had had an easier childhood than mine, despite the death of her father. Though I didn't understand class distinctions so clearly at the time, I had grown up in a working class home, and had learned to get by without most of the trappings of middle class life. I felt that, having learned how to do without as a kid, I could handle problems a lot better than the pampered middle class types could.

Around this time something new surfaced in the rock and roll scene — the artist who had *kicked the habit*. In the music business tradition of *any publicity is good publicity* the artist would give the interview talking about how he or she (usually he) had finally gotten off junk and about what a struggle it had been. The article would feature photos of the artist with a sleeveless shirt, holding his arms up at a concert, proudly showing off the skin that had no track marks. Maybe the new album would have similar sleeveless pictures on the jacket.

Even one of these articles was plenty for me. I thought, "Isn't this wonderful! You did something stupid for years and years. Lucky for you, you didn't kill yourself. Now you finally decided to stop being stupid. Good for you! Congratulations! You want a gold ribbon?"

Soon after reading the article, I would listen to the new album, and it was almost always a disappointment, usually being an uninspired rehash of past glories. I hadn't had much respect for junkies to begin with, and as time went on, I had even less, but I had to wonder why a junkie's music would suffer when he stopped shooting up. In my own experience, I felt that a musician's inspiration came from the core of his or her personality. Did this mean that all these junkies had no inspiration without junk, or had the drug simply sapped what had been there originally?

As the personal stories of so many junkie musicians unfolded in the 1970s, the tales moved on to the next chapter, which was almost predictable to someone like myself after my summer in 1971 on the Strip in Atlanta. A year of so after the junkie did his big announcement and did his *clean* album, he would go back to using. Then another year or two later, he'd kick again. Over and over. The story is probably as old as the drug, and even before my personal experience of knowing junkies in Atlanta, I had read about it in stories in high school. I knew that it was a rare junkie who actually quit for good. Even before knowing much about heroin, I had observed the same pattern with cigarettes, and while I didn't know what it felt like to be addicted to something, I could clearly see its power over people.

Here again, I thought that I had grown up stronger than others because I had to do so. I had to live without a lot of frills, so I learned to live that way, and I felt I didn't need some kind of crutch. I could deal with life's hard, cold realities without taking refuge in a bottle or a needle, and I didn't feel sorry for those who did. I thought they were largely a bunch of self-indulgent cry-babies who needed to grow up and get over whatever it was that was bothering them.

Of course, Neil Young had done his song *The Needle and the Damage Done* a few years earlier. Neil already knew the pain of losing a close friend and band mate to the needle, and over the next few years would lose at least one more friend to that damage done.

As the 1970s unfolded, so did Keith Richards' ongoing smack saga, and with each chapter, I had less and less respect for him. As far as I could tell, though, most of the rest of the Rolling Stones seemed untouched by the demon that had infected Keith. Having loved the Beatles from the first time I saw them on *The Ed Sullivan Show* back in February of 1964, I was glad that they had also largely bypassed the heroin monkey. John Lennon, who clearly had some issues going on in his head from an early age, had developed a smack addiction for a short period, but then had gotten off the drug, and apparently, unlike most addicts, never returned to it. From all indications, Paul, George and Ringo, if they had tried the drug at all, seemed to have never developed any interest in it.

I wondered how much of Keith's heroin addiction had to do with trying to live up to the *bad boy* image. The Beatles, being the *good* guys, didn't need to try to prove how bad they were. The Rolling Stones were a different story, though. Rock and roll, after all, wasn't supposed to be simply entertainment. The stories that the songwriters of the time told from the stage and on record were supposed to be true stories, meant to convey the thoughts and emotions of real experience. In theory, something really happened between Papa John (of The Mamas and The Papas) and the woman he was singing to in the song *Monday, Monday* and Bob Dylan had a real object of desire when he sang *I Want You*. Of course, this didn't mean that every song had a literal meaning or inspiration, and probably not many people thought Paul McCartney actually had a French lover named *Michelle*, but the general idea was that the music of the time conveyed genuine experience, and if it did not do so, it had little or no validity.

In the beginning, almost all of the songs were about love, lost or found, good or bad, but after a while many songwriters felt the need to expand their palettes and go beyond romance to perhaps something deeper and more profound. When Jimi Hendrix asked *Are You Experienced?* he made it clear that he was, and that experience included a trip through some *Purple Haze*. John Lennon had obviously seen *Lucy in the Sky With Diamonds* before writing the song, and you didn't need to think too hard to figure out how he found her. But if the Beatles and others found new inspiration and artistic direction from psychedelics, the Rolling Stones excursion into the same territory produced results that were mixed at best. They really connected much better when they made the move to the darker side, and when they sang "I've got nasty habits" and "I'm a Monkey Man" they conveyed a power that their *psychedelic* songs lacked.

Being bad was one thing when it meant keeping a lover *Under My Thumb* or complaining because *(I Can't Get No) Satisfaction* but quite another when the subject was drugs and their companion lifestyle. If you wanted to be the really bad boy, no doubt about it, heroin is and always was really bad, so as a matter of image, Keith's drug of choice made sense. As someone observing the process and looking at it in purely practical terms, I thought Keith's choice was foolish in the extreme. If it fueled his creativity, helping him write good songs and come up with cool guitar riffs, then he could do it, as far as I was concerned. But when the good songs and cool riffs became few and far between, I just thought he was needlessly wasting his life and his creativity. I saw the drug as initially giving him a creative high, just as it did physically, but then gradually robbing him of his talents, so that in the end he had no real inspiration left, with or without the drug. I felt very clearly that if I went down the road he had, I would end up that way, so this was how I judged him, and the facts seemed to support my conclusion.

Joni Mitchell had released a song in 1970 where, in speaking to her lover, she mentions that his circle of friends got involved with acid, grass, booze, guns and needles. She makes it clear that these things this circle did for *laughs* made her very uneasy. Only a couple of years later she would do a song that painted a much closer and more personal picture of the heroin lifestyle, though I never got any indications that she herself got too deeply into that addictive lifestyle. While I have no special sources for information one way or the other, I have the impression that she somehow avoided the curse that affected so many other famous and not-so-famous musicians of the era.

Significantly, Joni also did a song in the 1970s called *Trouble Child* about someone who is in a sterilized room, that being probably either a hospital or asylum. The trouble child in the song has attitudes that must be changed somehow and for some reason. I thought about my mother, who was the trouble child of our family. Was this the key to the problems? Did she have attitudes that she stubbornly refused to adjust? I had seen my mother in certain situations act in very stubborn ways, refusing to change her attitudes and act in a more responsible, *socially-acceptable* way. Could this be at the root cause of her schizophrenia, or was it simply a symptom of a deeper and more complex problem? And was it truly right, or even necessary, to make someone conform to the expected *norms* of society? Was Mom simply the very sharp square peg being forced into the round hole, with her edges being blunted and dulled by tranquilizers and other *soothing* medications? I knew my mother was an intelligent woman, and I wondered if some-how that had worked against her. And was it right to try to force someone to act in more responsible, socially-acceptable ways? And could it be that my mother's real problem was that she was too smart for her own good?

Some time in the middle of that summer of 1974 my wife and I returned to the Chicago area, only to split up. After that, I made some new musical friends in Evanston, including a pair of singer/songwriter bothers living at the house of an old college buddy. One of the brothers reminded me a bit of my partner from the strip in Atlanta a few years earlier, and the resemblance turned out to be more than physical appearance — he also had a little smack habit, as it turned out. The other brother, who I judged to be the more talented of the pair, was simply an alcoholic, as it turned out, as was the bass player who often played shows with them. I had come to the point of thinking that being an alcoholic musician didn't sound so bad, against the backdrop of an endless parade of junkies. By the time the whole *Sid and Nancy* thing happened in 1977, I felt like asking if they both became junkies just to prove to themselves and the world how creative they were. If so, just how stupid did they have to be to go down that path? Did you have to be this stupid to be a modern musician? I hoped not.

My new musical friends in Evanston introduced me to the wonders of pot brownies, which I found not so wonderful. As with my few other experiences with drugs, I felt no compelling reason to return for a repeat. I could enjoy an occasional glass of wine, but even after taking my first shot of Jack Daniels I felt I'd rather not do *that* again. As a low-level crook I met around this time said to me, "Getting high is not my thing." Clearly it wasn't mine either.

Throughout the 1970s, I met a lot of religious people on the street, from the Hari Krishna guys to the Moonies. In that era, religious groups commonly went fishing for new members on the street, and I also met a lot of people who had joined groups and then left them. Now having returned to Evanston,

I met one woman who had left the Church of Scientology, which had a center in Evanston, and she told me stories about the ways church members would come after her, trying to get her to return to the church. Her stories didn't surprise me, as they were very similar to tales of people I knew who had left other religious groups. What I didn't know then was the attitude that the Church of Scientology has regarding the field of psychiatry — they dismiss it entirely. Knowing *that* then would have truly surprised me. I might have questioned how much my mother's psychiatrist actually knew versus how much he was simply guessing at or trying to understand, but I did know that he knew at least a few things that I didn't.

At some point a while later, I discovered the writings of the Swiss psychologist Carl Jung. I had skimmed the surface of Sigmund Freud some time during high school, and I thought that his ideas made some sense but seemed to lack something, though I couldn't begin to say what that might be. Reading Jung, something major seemed to fall into place for me. Freud had identified the human sex drive as the strongest force at the core of the human psyche, but while it *is* a truly powerful motivator, Jung identified one other force as being even stronger and more powerful — specifically, the self-knowledge of mortality. Almost every human being born learns at a very young age that he or she will die, however long and well he or

Our cat Joker, with a prize in his mouth, on the porch of the house where my wife and I lived in Atlanta in the spring of 1974.

she might live, and human beings may be the only animal to carry that kind of self-knowledge. It seemed to me that while Freud was correct in emphasizing the importance of sex, Jung was even more correct in emphasizing the greater importance of the knowledge of one's own eventual death.

Freud and Jung, sex and death — the two most powerful urges within the depths of the human mind, and also the two subjects that the Doors covered so well in their music from the late 1960s and early 1970s. Freud, Jung and their colleagues had illuminated some of the layers in the texture of the human mind, and had greatly expanded our knowledge about what goes on inside a person's head, particularly with people who had mental problems.

From Jung's writing, I discovered the poem *Diagnosis* by Marcia Lee Anderson, which ends with the lines, "To know how simple is our deepest need/ How sharp, and how impossible to feed." Through my interest in Jung I also learned about an article called *Schizophrenia and the inevitability of death* by Dr. Harold F. Searles that had been published in 1961. Dr. Searles made a case, in his study, for the idea that at the root of schizophrenia one could find an elaborate mental self-defense mechanism for avoiding the knowledge of death. While I couldn't evaluate Dr. Searles' theory at the time, I could believe it, as it seemed quite sensible, and could explain much of what I had already observed. The argument gave me a simple way of understanding my mother's mental issues, and possibly my older brother's ones as well, allowing me to dismiss their problems and move on with my life without having to think about them.

I didn't personally fear death, though I had when I was a child. My wife's mother had once said to me, "When you die, it's over — that's the end." I thought she probably was right, though I could never say so with the kind of certainty that she had. I did think, though, that if death was the end, then there was no reason to fear it. If no pain or eternal damnation followed death, then why fear it? A person could fear the unknown, because it's unknown, but if nothing follows death, then there is nothing to fear.

From reading Jung and others such as Dr. Searles, I thought I had reached a workable understanding of my family's mental problems. I wasn't that closely involved with them at the time, either, so having satisfied my need to have an explanation for those mental issues, I didn't intend to give those issues much more concern. I thought I knew what I needed to know about them, when in reality I understood very little. I didn't go looking for increased understanding of psychiatry, but it would come my way, bit by bit, even though I wasn't looking.

Chapter 8

My Housemate B

I met my housemate B soon after I moved to Oakland, California in the summer of 1978, and I knew him as a fellow singer/songwriter for a couple of years before I moved into his house in Berkeley in September of 1981, but I hadn't known him quite as well as I soon would. In sharing the same living space, I soon realized that B was an alcoholic. I knew that he dabbled in other so-called *recreational drugs* as well, and had a real fondness for cocaine, but I could also tell that he at least did not have a heroin habit. However, I was never sure about the possibility of him turning into a junkie. He admitted to me that he liked heroin, so I didn't know how much further he'd have to go down that slippery slope before he reached the point of no return.

I told B, in our conversations, about seeing the guy nodding out in the alleyway on the strip in Atlanta, and I told him that it didn't look like fun to me, laying in an alleyway. B's reply to me was, "Yeah, but he feels so good he doesn't care." I found that statement a bit disturbing. Of course, no matter how bad a person's situation is, he could always find a temporary escape in some sort of drug. It's also true that the human mind does sometimes have a need to escape from reality, and people who don't escape through drugs or alcohol find refuge in movies, TV, tabloid celebrity gossip, video games or hobbies that offer some sort of route to fantasy. However, at the end of the escape route is the return to reality, and won't the guy in the alleyway have to eventually face the fact that he's lying in an alleyway? If he takes another shot, he can temporarily feel better again, but each time he does, isn't he simply postponing the inevitable? Taking the drug doesn't make his reality better, no matter how good it makes him feel, and in fact it makes his reality worse, so as a purely practical matter, wouldn't he be better off facing his reality sooner than later?

I also wondered about a possible connection with religion to all of this. Marx had called religion *the opiate of the people* and perhaps those who could no longer believe in religion simply moved to another opiate. Having left the Christian religion, I tried not to judge those who continued to believe what I no longer could, but I wondered if the lack of religion among many in my own generation might account for the more widespread drug use. Walking along the Berkeley streets near my home one day, I stepped along a section of the sidewalk where someone had written in chalk a version of the Baudelaire quote: "Be drunk always, with wine, with poetry, or with virtue, as you will." I liked that quote. I understood that I personally had chosen a modern form of poetry, called *rock and roll*, as my preferred form of drunkenness, and that for me it was enough. I also understood that for many rock and roll musicians it wasn't enough, though I didn't understand why.

When I told B that I had no interest in drugs, he said, "You've got to get into drugs! Drugs are great — they're like sex with woman, but without the rejection!" So was that it? Was it that simple? Were all these junkie musicians shooting up because they couldn't handle the way women had put them down? I could see where some of that could play a part, but on the whole, it didn't seem to work as a major explanation. I had already gotten plenty of rejection from women by then, and I knew that the best way to get past that rejection was to find another potential mate. While my list of possibilities might be very short, I knew that some of these big-time rockers had very long lists. Could a famous musician's ego be so fragile that rejection by one woman couldn't be soothed by the comfort of one or more of the hundreds of other possibilities? Maybe sometimes it happened that way, but I didn't think it happened very often.

I read the current research about brain chemistry, and it did seem to agree with B at least a little, though. The researchers identified the human body's natural pain killers, and explained that when those were in short supply, even the simplest body movements would become extremely painful. Morphine and heroin were originally created as pain killers to bring comfort to soldiers in extreme pain due to their war wounds. When someone not in pain takes the drug for the first time, it makes the user feel very good the first time, but the body's balancing mechanism also kicks in, noting the presence of an over-supply of pain killer. If someone continues to use the drug, they soon become dependent on the external pain killer as the body reduces its output of internal pain killers to compensate for the over-abundance that it detects. Soon, the user needs the external drug to simply function, and without it will be in extreme pain. The user may then increase the dosage, looking for that original high, and the cycle will repeat itself as the user gets drawn in deeper and deeper. If the user keeps increasing the dose, that user may die of an overdose, and for some, this happened very early in the cycle, maybe even at the second round, though as I noted in the Atlanta chapter, there are plenty of other ways for a junkie to die as well.

Beyond the physical mechanism of addiction, though, what about the psychological or psychiatric connection? Researchers noted at the time that moments of pleasure trigger the release of natural pain killers in the brain, so when something happened to make someone feel happy, their brain would trigger a release of those internal drugs. If you get a nice check in the mail, that could make you feel good, but for a lot of people, nothing feels as good as love and what a lover can do. Understanding how this works, I thought that maybe B was more right than not, but I really couldn't say. It didn't change my attitude about junkies at all, though — if that was the real problem, that those guys just couldn't get over how some woman put them down, they needed to grow up, pull themselves together and figure out how to get over it. Life deals everyone a certain set of hands, and no matter who you are, some of those hands will be bad — that's simply the luck of the draw, and no one wins every time. In fact, most of these guys were winning a lot more than me, so why couldn't they handle a bad card every now and then? Or was that it — did they get used to winning so much that they just couldn't handle a serious loss? And if that was the case, why should I feel sorry for any of them? Well, quite honestly, at the time I didn't feel sorry for any of them.

A little while before moving into B's house, and for some time after, I started recording a series of songs with a guy named Michael who lived in Alameda. Michael had a very good set of ears, and his talents had been recognized by a significant selection of musical professionals in L.A. In fact, Michael had such a good reputation that he managed to do what so many Bay Area musicians wished they could figure out how to do — he made a very good income from the L.A. scene while living in Northern California.

Making recordings together in the early 1980s, I very quickly learned to appreciate Michael's talents. He was the lead sound man for a number of famous musicians, and he got paid well to make them sound good for their live shows, or at least, that's what I thought he got paid to do. He was, without question, a sound expert, and every night on the job, he made the band sound as good as they possibly could, and he solved each and every sound equipment problem that came along, big or small, with the innate ability of someone who made the job look easy when, very often, it probably wasn't. When you hired Michael, you knew he could and would take care of everything sound-wise, and you could trust his judgement — if Michael told you he needed part *B* then you would send the roadie out to get it, and when he got back with the part, Michael would have it installed and get everything back up and running before you could even believe it. Michael had the wizard's touch at the sound board, as someone who knows and likes what he's doing, and I thought that was what he did for all those famous L.A. musicians.

Actually, it was part of what he did for those guys, but it wasn't all there was to the job. I would ask him occasionally how things were going, and how the shows had been with this or that artist. He never wanted to talk about it. Why? Was it because it had become so routine to him that he was bored by the whole thing? What was really going on here?

Well, at some point a few years later, he couldn't take it any more. He quit the whole L.A. scene and made it clear to all of his former connections that he was done for good. Not long after he made that decision, I visited him at his new job, behind the desk at a car rental agency. This I *really* didn't understand. He had given up a well-paying job for which he had remarkable skill and passion so that he could work a low-paying unskilled job that anyone could do. Why?

Michael looked at me and answered before I even had the chance to ask the question, and he said it as if it was the most obvious answer of all. "Dave," he said, "I just got tired of playing nursemaid for junkies." So that was it. His ability to do the job well wasn't enough for all these famous guys he worked for. Most of them were jerks, as it turned out, caught up in their own little junkie worlds, who expected him to not just do his job well, but to kiss butt to them in a hundred different ways, and to, as he put it, "wipe their butts and replace their diapers." He took the load they piled on him for as long as he could, but finally his dignity could stand no more, and I understood. The stories just added to my accumulated loathing for junkie musicians in general, and knowing which ones were junkies lowered my personal artistic respect for them each by a notch or two.

My housemate B, meanwhile, had taken a job in Berkeley with Cal Performances, and had developed his skills as a stage hand. Working closely with star musicians, stage hands get to see the real person behind the star persona, and B mentioned more than once that working as a stage hand would cure anyone of being *star struck*. His comment didn't surprise me, because by then I had very few cherished illusions left about the musicians who made the music I loved.

I did have at least one illusion left, though, and B shattered it. He told me that he had walked in on a certain famous artist shooting up in a backstage bathroom. I thought, "No, not him too!" I had gotten used to finding out that this or that guy was a junkie, but I had cherished the illusion that this one particular artist, whatever other drugs he might have done, was not a junkie. I knew B didn't make up stories, though, and while I tried to find some way to explain it away and somehow rebuild that cherished fantasy, I couldn't. Yes, that guy too was a junkie.

I still remained committed to the idea that you could be a creative musician and not be a junkie. In 1979 I had met Jeff Larson after hearing him on a small San Francisco stage, and he and I quickly became friends. Jeff had, even at the age of 18, one of the most amazing singing voices I had ever heard, along with a developing songwriting style that I liked a lot. Over the next few years we tried working together a few times, both on stage and in a recording setting, with varying degrees of success, and we called our duo either Dusty River (my idea) or Northern Pacific (his idea, which I actually liked better than my own). While our partnership never quite worked out, we remained close friends and would often get together whenever possible to swap riffs and song ideas.

Jeff had, like myself, wondered at a young age whether he might end up as a junkie, simply due to his attraction to music. However, like me as well, he never chose to take any steps in that direction, and he never had any interest in doing so. In fact, one of the things that drew us together as musicians, in addition to our mutual interest in music of a certain type, was our mutual determination to avoid the whole drug scene, and we shared similar attitudes about it which only deepened over time.

I developed close friendships with a few other Bay Area musicians who also felt the same way. I met a bass player from Oakland named Clive, and a lead guitar player from Oakland named Brad, and for a while we tried to put together a rock and roll band. While the band ultimately never quite came together, the one thing we all shared, and which we would speak of often in the next few years as we remained friends, was our mutual disdain for the drugged-out stupidity of so many of our fellow musicians. None of us needed the sauce, no matter what was in the brew, and we didn't think too highly of those who did. Those people had all gotten themselves into some trouble of their own making and we were all sensible enough and knew enough not to go looking for trouble.

Brad and Clive had both met my housemate B, and they felt much the same way about him as I did. They liked his music, his songwriting, his singing, his recording, his musicianship and his whole creative angle, but they found his personality a bit scratchy at the edges. B seemed like a guy only about halfway together, who might fall apart at any moment, and the other guys wondered how I managed to share a house with him. In the long run, B never fell apart, but he never got himself any more together either.

B had told me during our years in the house in Berkeley that drugs and/or alcohol would improve my writing, and that he never wrote songs without being high or buzzed. I told him I didn't think it would work for me. I had only tried writing once or twice after having a bit of alcohol, and it only confused me. I didn't find any additional inspiration from the alcohol, and I didn't come up with anything worth saving. I told B that his method seemed to work well for him, but it did nothing for me. B didn't even seem to get the idea that his way of writing might not work for me. I liked his writing, and I would not have tried to tell him that he should try to write songs my way. I did not think he was necessarily having a good life, being an alcoholic, but I had to admit that it worked for him creatively, and since I liked what he did that way, maybe it was all right that he was an alcoholic. I also had to admit to myself that if I needed alcohol to feed my creativity, then maybe I would choose to be an alcoholic too. Like every other creative person I've know in my life, I care more about that process than just about anything else, and I would do whatever I needed to do to fuel that process. Fortunately for me, I didn't need alcohol or any other chemicals to help me write songs.

I also read a writer in a local paper, during this era, who wrote an article in which he included the phrase "not for nothing does someone put a needle into their arm." I wondered about that statement. The writer seemed to be saying that people who shoot heroin have some compelling reason for doing so. but he didn't say what that reason might be, and I myself did not have any kind of answer for that one, simply vague guesses.

Chapter 9

The Cuckoo's Nest

I don't know Jack, and I admit that. Of course I don't know him personally, but I also don't know the celebrity gossip on him, either. Maybe he beats his maid and pays her less than minimum wage, or maybe he pays her a living wage and gives her extra days off. For all I know, maybe Jack doesn't even have a maid. Being a musician myself, I always paid more attention to, say, who the current members of Fleetwood Mac happened to be, and who they hooked up with, so I didn't spend much time on stories about Hollywood actors.

One thing I do know about Jack, though, and that I knew from the moment I saw his character lighting up the screen in *Easy Rider*, is that Jack cares about his craft. When you see Jack play a role, you can take it to the bank, and not just in the way the studio does on their balance sheet — you can believe it. Jack is, in the moments you watch, living the part he portrays, as if he *is* the person you see on the screen.

When I walked into the Berkeley theatre to see *One Flew Over the Cuckoo's Nest* I didn't know the story I was about to see. I hadn't read the book, although I did know its reputation, and I knew that its author Ken Kesey had based his fiction story on real experiences and observations working on the late shift at an insane asylum during his college years. The story seemed a bit lightweight to me at the beginning, but of course it was drawing me in, along with the rest of the theatre audience, and once drawn in, it took us all step by step to one of the most gut-wrenching climaxes in the entire history of cinema, followed by a short and necessary anti-climax to give the audience a much-needed small ray of hope before they left the theatre after witnessing such heavy, dark despair.

On the way to that gut-wrenching climax, however, Jack plays an earlier scene that had an even deeper impact on me personally. According to the movie story line, Jack's character is about to be punished for bad behavior in the asylum, and his punishment will be a shock treatment. I can never forget the look of fear in my mother's eyes when my grandmother would threaten to have her taken up to the State Hospital for shock treatments if she didn't behave.

As I watched Jack's character being tied up, I thought about what an interesting little side benefit I was about to receive. I had come to the theatre expecting to experience a story that would entertain, instruct and/or move me in some way, but I hadn't expected to see a realistic portrayal of what my mother had experienced. I thought this would be very interesting indeed.

Actually, Jack's portrayal of a patient on the receiving end of a shock treatment hit me harder than any other cultural moment in my life, far beyond any other movie, song, play, book or anything else could do. As undeniably powerful as the climax of *Cuckoo's Nest* is, I had already experienced the personal gut-wrench in the shock treatment scene. When I left the theatre that night, I wondered if younger brother had seen *Cuckoo's Nest* and I knew that whenever he saw it, he would feel the same way I did about the shock treatment scene. When we spoke about it a few years later he confirmed this and said that when he saw it, he thought the same thing about me that I did about him.

Some time shortly after seeing *Cuckoo's Nest*, I met someone on the street collecting signatures for a petition, which was a common occurrence at the time. I often signed petitions on the street in Berkeley, because usually I agreed with those petitions. In this case, though, I felt my agreement was not at 60%, or even 90%, but more like 2000%. The petition sought to have shock treatments classified as *cruel and unusual punishment* and to have them banned from further use. I wished at that moment that I could be ten people signing that petition, and I wished the petitioner well in her quest to end the practice.

As a brief side note regarding shock treatments, I want to make it clear that I think the treatment originated from a genuine desire to help people who needed help, and I don't fault psychiatrists who, in the 1950s and 1960s, had limited knowledge and understanding of the psychiatric problems their patients faced. They undoubtedly felt the need to try to do something to help their patients, and in the human trial-and-error method of learning, I put the shock treatment in the category of a necessary error in that time period. It didn't achieve its stated and hoped-for goal, but it brought greater understanding. The abuse of the treatment, as portrayed in *Cuckoo's Nest*, is an unfortunate but all-too-common side effect of human situations where one person has absolute and unaccountable control over others, and I know it's possible that my mother experienced some of that same brand of cruelty that Jack's character did in the movie. I did not follow the further development of the shock treatment procedure from the 1980s onward, but in the early years of the twenty-first century, my mother once again experienced a schizophrenic episode that required hospital confinement, and then I got an update on the story. During this hospital stay I learned that she had received shock treatments. Knowing this, I asked her about the new shock treatments, and she told me that they didn't hurt her at all, and that they actually seemed to help. The answer surprised me, and I was pleased to learn that some time during the previous two decades the procedure had evolved into a method of actually helping psychiatric patients, though my mother couldn't say when that happened. She did make it very clear to me, though, that modern shock treatments were nothing like the bad old days.

On the streets of Berkeley, around the time that I saw *Cuckoo's Nest*, a lot of homeless people began showing up. To get more money for the wealthy, Ronald Reagan essentially eliminated federal funding for insane asylums. Our society had, in an earlier era, constructed places for people with mental problems, and as *Cuckoo's Nest* made clear, some of those charged with caring for and helping those patients acted as petty dictators and abused those they were supposed to help. Knowing this, some may have at first celebrated the act of opening the doors of the asylums and letting the patients go free. However, when the real world consequences of the change showed up on the streets of Berkeley soon afterwards, no one in town felt it deserved celebration.

President Reagan, in cutting the funding for mental institutions, was saying, in effect, that we as a society and a nation now had no responsibility to look after people with mental problems. These people would now have to get help from family if they had family, and if not, they would now be on their own. Individual states had usually operated most of the mental institutions but they had depended on federal funding for their continued existence, and without it, most of them closed their doors or down-sized themselves to near non-existence.

So Berkeley, being the kind of place that welcomes the unwelcome and that tries to help the helpless, became the destination for some very troubled people who had nowhere to go. A lot of former asylum inmates began living on the streets of Berkeley during this time. Given the antagonism that had existed between Reagan and Berkeley during his years as California governor some two decades earlier, perhaps this was Reagan's ultimate revenge.

A few years later, when Reagan said that most of the homeless chose to be so, I didn't have an answer to that. Reagan's little self-serving excuse for the explosion of homelessness that his policy had caused didn't sound right to me, in light of what I'd seen over the years on the streets of Berkeley, but I still couldn't put together an adequate reply. When I heard someone suggest that perhaps there were human spirits that had to fly so high and free that the conventions of so-called *normal human behavior* could not effectively constrain them, it sounded poetic, but didn't seem to match most of the homeless people I saw on the streets.

One of the Berkeley street guys I remember was the *Windows on Behavior* guy. My Oakland friend Doug had given him that nickname after hearing him use the phrase. The *WOB* guy walked up and down the Berkeley streets in the area on the south side of the University of California campus, always talking loudly, as if announcing to the world rather than speaking to anyone in particular. He rarely stopped talking, and whatever came out of his mouth rarely made any logical sense but could be quite engaging in a stream-of-consciousness sort of way. Still, he didn't seem to be a high-flying free spirit — he looked to me like someone who needed help.

Early one Sunday morning my housemate B and I both woke up to the sound of someone out on the street saying the n-word loudly and endlessly. We both decided to find out who this jerk was, and we walked out of the house and went looking for him. We didn't have to go far to find him, and we had no trouble locating him from the sound of his voice, but when we got a good look at him we both realized he was yet another Berkeley *street crazy*, and we knew trying to talk to him would do no good. Somehow, he also didn't look like someone who had made a choice about living on the street.

In those years in Berkeley, I could not understand these troubled street people, and I could not have advocated for them in any real sense. I didn't know how these people had been treated in the asylums, though I was sure that some of them had been abused. But were they better off now, living on the streets of Berkeley? I didn't think so.

Chapter 10

Closer to Home

At the end of the summer of 1988, I filled a van with everything I had accumulated from a decade in Oakland and Berkeley that I could reasonably take with me, and I headed back East to be closer to the family. I found a place to live in Brooklyn, which put me about a four-hour drive away from the Binghamton area, so I could visit about every three or four weeks or so, and I could be close by, if and when a crisis occurred, as I knew some would.

Within that first year back on the East Coast, Mom would find herself in the psychiatric unit of Wilson Memorial Hospital in Johnson City, the place where she'd given birth to me nearly four decades earlier, and also the place where my younger brother had been born. Younger brother had moved back to the area shortly before me, after we both noted in a visit over the summer of 1987 that the grandmother we had grown up with seemed to be declining rapidly.

Mom would be in the psychiatric unit for two to three weeks, and so when I drove my van up from NYC to visit the family, I went over to see her with younger brother. He and I had already compared notes on our personal experiences with *One Flew Over the Cuckoo's Nest.* Now seeing her in the psychiatric ward, I thought about the movie, and I wondered about Mom. During this time, younger brother and I began to try to seriously understand Mom more than we had before, but for a long time we would not have clear answers to our questions.

I remembered the scene where McMurphy (Jack's character) tells the other patients that they're not really crazy, they just think they are. I wondered if that could be true about

Mom. For most of her life, she'd been told that she was crazy. How much of her craziness might be learned behavior? I knew she had been heavily medicated for most of her adult life, and I also knew that underneath that medication was a woman who rarely had had a chance to shine. When I looked into her eyes on that visit in 1989, I could see nothing that told me she was crazy. She looked all right, and acted all right, although a bit inhibited.

What did it mean to have schizophrenia? A couple of years earlier, one of my California singer/songwriter friends named Jim Bruno looked at me and said, "Roses are red, violets are blue, I'm a little schizzed and so am I." I didn't want to spoil his little joke at the time, so I didn't bother to tell him that schizophrenia is not multiple-personality disorder. People commonly confuse the two, but I knew that being *schizzed* did not mean having two or more people inside the same head, it meant that you heard voices in your head.

What does it mean to hear voices in you head? Doesn't everyone hear voices in their head? The human brain is not a monolith, after all — it has two sides, which constantly talk to, and sometimes fight with, each other. It has multiple layers and dimensions which add various shadings to the conversation. The human brain is, to say the least, a very complicated machine, which defies easy understanding.

I had heard this phrase about *hearing voices in your head* for much of my life, and I thought, up to this point, that it referred to the internal conversations that happened in someone's mind. A few years later, on a short visit to the Grand Canyon, I would stand at a place on the South Rim, admiring the view across that great expanse of jagged rock, and one of those internal voices in my mind would say, "If you believe strongly enough in yourself that you can fly, you can jump over this fence and you won't fall, you'll simply float through the air." Thoughts like that come from what I like to refer to as the *stupid part* of the brain. Psychiatrists and others who study brain activity may have a better and more descriptive term for this part of the human thought process. I commonly have such stupid and crazy passing thoughts, and most of the time I think I know better than to give much credence to them, or at least, I hope I do. In the case of the South Rim, the smarter side of my brain answered with "Yeah, right..."

A bit more disturbing are the passing thoughts of random and senseless violence. Having lived as long as I have, I carry the memory of small things I did or said many years ago that hurt someone unnecessarily, and I wish that I hadn't said or done what I did. However, as far as I know, I never caused anyone serious physical harm, and I know how much such an act would haunt me. Knowing that thoughts of violence are not *like me* in any real sense, I wonder where they come from. When I wake up from a dream where I shoot a gun randomly at passing cars, I'm relieved to realize it was just a dream, but I wonder why I would dream such a thing. Fortunately for me, such dreams are rare, and I know they don't represent hidden desires or anything like that.

I've also wondered if perhaps sometimes violent thoughts come from other people around a person. I remember that I had a lot more of these strange violent thoughts while living in New York City than I ever did living anywhere else. I wondered if perhaps the thought of throwing someone in front of an oncoming subway train came from the mind of someone else looking at me and imagining me doing that, and, not knowing me, perhaps wondering if I could be the kind of person who could do that. I do think that sometimes other people can put thoughts into a person's head, though I certainly don't claim to know how *that* works, and whether or not it has been studied or even could be studied with present technology.

So I know that I have a lot of crazy stuff floating around at the edges of my mind, and I don't give that stuff much room on the main stage of my conscious thought process. I have, for most of my life, imagined that most people have similar strange conversations in their minds. I had come to understand, by mid-1989, that psychiatrists had at that time identified a few types of schizophrenics, and my mother was a *disorganized schizophrenic*. Most people, if they know anything about schizophrenia, know about the *paranoid schizophrenics*. These people may sometimes do violence to other people, and I thought that perhaps they listened to, and gave credence and conscious thought to, the violent internal thoughts that I dismissed out of hand. My mother being a disorganized schizophrenic, maybe she gave in to the crazy thoughts — not the ones about jumping off a cliff, but maybe just down to the next notch of *crazy*.

In 1989 this was the extent of my understanding of schizophrenia. I did not understand why my mother, who was certainly an intelligent woman, would give credence to the kind of crazy thoughts in her head that I would immediately dismiss when they bubbled up. Why did she *go off the edge*, and why did she have a hard time getting back to the shallow end of the pool? My father and the grandparents seemed to have an idea that this expressed some weakness in her character. As my grandfather said many times, "It's all in the mind." Why couldn't she simply pull herself together, get up and over it, and stop listening to those crazy ideas in her mind? And how much of this came from her real mother? That woman hadn't raised her, but maybe she had influenced her somehow. Maybe on those visits to Freeville those two were reinforcing each others' craziness — was that possible?

Younger brother and I couldn't answer those questions at the time, but we also knew that something didn't quite add up. We started asking her more questions, in the hope of better understanding, though initially the answers just made us more confused. Older brother was not part of this process — he didn't seem to care about understanding her, he just tried to get along day to day living with her.

During another visit to the old family home, as the family gathered for lunch in the kitchen, Mom appeared wearing headphones. She was listening to music, and singing along in a weird sort of way, off-key and partly mumbling. I'd encountered this phenomenon previously on the subway in NYC, and found the sound of someone doing this highly annoying. I found it not much less annoying to hear my own mother doing it in the kitchen of the family home. My grandfather explained that Mom's psychiatrist had recommended that she try listening to headphones as a way of drowning out some of the voices in her head, and so she was trying. He of course thought the whole idea was ridiculous, and he repeated his line that "It's all in the mind."

The conflict between the two of them smoldered just beneath the surface that day, and did not erupt into any angry outbursts, but it was always present. I felt saddened then by the dynamic that played out between them, and I knew it would continue until one of them died, most likely him. For most of the time they had shared the same house, this conflict had continued.

Part of the root of the problem lay in the unstated idea that Mom had somehow, and for some reason, chosen to be the *bad* girl. In church sometimes Mom would hear someone cough or clear their throat, and she would react as if somehow this gesture was aimed at her, which embarrassed all the rest of us. For the few other occasions when the family ventured out together in public other than church, maybe to visit the State Fair in Syracuse or the Corning Glass Works, we always kept watch to see how and if Mom would embarrass us.

The unstated but understood idea was that Mom could make herself be all right if she simply chose to do so, but due to some flaw in her character, she stubbornly clung to her strange ideas and her weakness. "It's all in the mind," seemed to imply that she could simply somehow change her mind for the better.

As I said in the introduction, imagine a man with an invisible broken arm, who looks to be in good physical shape. Now, imagine that you need to have this man do pushups. No matter how you try to get him to do it, he can't, whether you yell at him, offer to pay him, whip him or give him donuts. Be nice to him, be angry with him, be hard or soft with him, nothing will work. You tell him he could to those pushups if he believes strongly enough in his own ability to do them, but even if he believes you, or tries to, he still cannot do those pushups. He complains of the intense pain of his efforts, and you call him a cry-baby. You have no doubt that he can do those pushups, but all he does is wimp out and complain about some pain he claims to have.

I saw some variation of this sad dynamic play out through all of my childhood between my mother and the couple who had adopted her, and it continued for much of the time that they still lived. Not really understanding, I thought the older folks were probably right, but I also hoped that when they were gone that my mother could have a more peaceful life. As it turned out, there was less conflict with the older folks gone, but life is rarely if ever peaceful for a schizophrenic.

While younger brother and I struggled to understand Mom at the time, though, one other mystery became very clear to him and me. He had moved into a rooming house in Endicott, and among the other roomers there was my old childhood friend D. The two of them started spending time together, and D soon told younger brother the missing puzzle piece — D's father had died of Huntington's Disease.

I knew about Huntington's Disease from reading about how it struck its most famous victim, Woody Guthrie. At the root of all the singer/songwriters that I discovered in the early

1970s was a man who had planted the seeds of the whole garden a few decades earlier, that original singer/songwriter named Woody. You couldn't read the biography of Bob Dylan's early career in New York City without touching on the connection with Woody, and Woody's illness.

Huntington's Disease doesn't require a long explanation — it's a degenerative brain disease, and when a person with Huntington's has children, about one of every two will end up with it as well. D's father may have already known he had the disease when he dropped the paint brush, but in 1960 people didn't usually admit such things to their neighbors. I believe that even then the genetic origin of the disease was understood, but perhaps some might have been embarrassed by the disease because of the implication that maybe having the disease meant they carried *bad genes*.

Knowing that D's father died of Huntington's Disease explained the mystery about D. From his early adulthood, D had known that he carried the same early death sentence as his father, and having seen his father slowly fall apart, he knew just what to expect. D and I would see each other one more time, but at that point we didn't know what to say to each other. I could say nothing to lighten the dark cloud hanging over him, and sharing old childhood memories seemed pointless in the face of the present reality he lived with every day. Not long after, he disappeared and someone died jumping off a bridge in Owego. While the body wasn't positively identified as his, younger brother and I felt sure that it was him.

Now being closer to home, I was beginning to put together pieces of the past, but it would still take almost a decade to come to the real understanding of the mystery that began at age three and a half.

Another year or two later, in the winter of 1992, I had a brief personal experience with the mechanics of drug addiction. I awoke one morning with an odd physical condition that I had never heard of, and my doctor explained that Western medicine identified this ailment hundreds of years ago but has yet to clearly understand the root causes. Western medicine also does not yet have a genuine cure for the problem, but I got the usual prescription handed out to treat this sickness, which was a steroid.

During the weeks that I took this steroid, I felt a high overall energy level, and a noticeably more aggressive general attitude. I could easily see how sports professionals would find steroids attractive, and the stories I heard and read which mentioned various sports celebrities in the context of rumored steroid use or abuse did not surprise me. When I reached the

From right to left, my father, the woman who raised my mother and my mother's real mother, some time during the 1980s. From looking at this photo, you would probably not guess that the woman on the left would outlive the other two.

end of the steroid treatment of my illness, I went through a gradual step-down process which ended with taking half of a pill for two days before taking none at all. I still had a few pills left in the prescription bottle, and on the first day with no pills, I woke up feeling bad and felt awful for the entire day. I knew, for that entire day, that to go from feeling very bad to feeling very good, all I would have had to do was to take another half of a pill. From that short experience alone, I easily understood the temptation to continue the drug use. I didn't do it, and the next day I felt fine, although I lacked that magical high energy level and more aggressive attitude, but I also never forgot just how badly I felt on the first day without the drug.

Chapter 11

Kurt Crying Out

In the early months of 1994, the Kurt Cobain tragedy began to unfold. I generally liked Nirvana, though I wouldn't have called myself a major fan of their music. I liked a lot of their songs, though they had some I didn't care about. I also understood the band's place at the head of the Seattle *grunge music* scene, and I agreed with the music critics who credited the grunge bands with revitalizing the largely lackluster American music landscape of the late 1980s.

So I appreciated Cobain's talent, but I didn't expect him to ever achieve the kind of status that 1960s musicians like Steve Stills or Eric Clapton had. I didn't follow his career the way I once had done with Stills and Clapton, so his personal trauma didn't mean as much to me. I didn't care to hear about it, but listening to rock and roll radio at the time, I did hear about it whether I wanted to or not.

At some point in early 1994 Cobain attempted suicide and ended up in a hospital. The rock station I listened to played a tape of him speaking with his wife, Courtney Love, from his bedside, and he said, "What is there left to live for?" From the sound of his voice, he seemed to be crying as he asked the question.

"WHAT IS THERE LEFT TO LIVE FOR?" As I listened to that tape, my gut reaction was one not of sympathy or concern, but of utter disgust. I could have been a Marine drill sergeant standing in his room. I imagined myself, as that drill sergeant, slapping Cobain around and screaming, "Wake up, you fool! You've got a newborn daughter that your wife just gave birth to — if nothing else, you've got a very real responsibility to do the best for her you possibly can for at least the next two or three decades! Then there's your beautiful wife, who obviously loves you very much! And on top of that, you as a musician have achieved the kind of acclaim in your career that millions of other musicians can only dream of! Snap out of it! Be thankful for what you've got, and appreciate it for what it is! Stop whining, you stupid cry-baby!"

I couldn't feel sorry for Kurt, and I didn't want to hear about him feeling sorry for himself. As the details of his story emerged, as usual, junk figured into the equation, as it so often does, and it gave me one more reason to not care about him. I saw him then as simply one more cry-baby junkie in a long line of musician cry-baby junkies. I could respect him for the creative things he did which I liked, but I couldn't respect him personally as an addict.

I knew about a Nirvana song called *Lithium* and I guessed that this drug also figured into the equation in some way. Around this time I met a fellow musician who also took lithium, though I didn't ask him anything about it. He had become a big fan of my music, and when I visited him I learned that he still lived in his parents' house, even though he was at least my age and probably a few years older, and he didn't seem to have any sort of job or income. I wondered how long that situation would continue, and what he would do when his parents passed on. I also wondered what his parents thought of him, and how they related to their son.

The closing chapter of Cobain's final tragedy came in the early spring of 1994, as he succeeded in killing himself. I felt no more sympathy for Kurt than I had for Sylvia Path or so many other suicides, though I did feel sorry for Kurt's daughter, who would now have to grow up without her father, a man who she would never really know.

I heard people speculate about the pressures of success and/or the fear of success when they spoke of Cobain, and I couldn't buy it. I had heard the argument before, in similar situations, and I had given it some consideration a couple of decades earlier, but by the time of Cobain's death I had long since dismissed that discussion. In those two decades I had seen a lot of people work very hard to succeed, but I had never met anyone who actually feared success, so I couldn't imagine *that* situation. I had read stories of people who worked hard to succeed, and who then turned around and destroyed that success, but this *fear of success/pressure of success* theory sounded to me like someone reaching for a simple explanation to cover a case that was in reality not so simple. I didn't know him personally, but I didn't believe that Kurt Cobain feared his own success, or that he lacked confidence in his own musical abilities related to his career going forward. To paraphrase an old Bogart line, I never knew of a musician who had talent and didn't know it, and some give themselves credit for more than what they've got.

Little did I know, at the time of Cobain's death, that I would someday in only a few short years stand next to someone and hear that person say the exact same thing that Kurt had said, and in exactly the same tone of voice — "What is there left to live for?" At that moment I would need an answer to that question, but I would also understand this mystery of Mr. Cobain, and so many others, that I had so easily dismissed out of my own ignorance.

Chapter 12

Can Staten Island Cause Depression?

In the summer of 1994 I began dating a woman who I'll call M, for the sake of her privacy. She and I had known each other a few years earlier, and a chance meeting let to a date, and that date led to the beginning of a romance. On the night of that first date, we shared a meal in a Manhattan restaurant, and later in the evening, at my apartment, she mentioned that she had to take her medication. Medication for what? Depression.

My first thought, in hearing the answer, was that I really didn't know what I was getting into. Only a year or two earlier, I had heard Bonnie Raitt sing a song about how she didn't need to get involved romantically with someone who has problems, and I strongly agreed. I felt my life had enough complications without adding any more wrinkles, but here I was. I felt that I'd have to be careful with this possible romance, and watch every step along the way.

In the early stages, as I looked for possible problems, I found none. We got along well and we enjoyed each other's company. Whatever disagreements or arguments we had all fit within the context of the beginning of a relationship. I looked for big bumps or bends in the road, and none came along. I didn't claim to understand M's depression, but it didn't seem to cause her any great problems. She explained to me, in due time, that she'd been taking her depression medication for a few years, and that it mostly took care of her condition. She also saw a therapist for forty minutes once a week, and the sessions helped her as well.

I made the mistake, early on, of looking for some sort of cause for her depression. M had a sad history with her former lovers which included more than one who had violently mistreated her, and she also had had a rough life trying to survive in New York City as an artist and painter. M had plenty of reasons to feel sad, and I tried to not give her any more. M was also the only one of her high school quartet of friends who had no major achievements to show for her adult life. Her three high school friends had each made impressive careers for themselves in the two decades since graduation, and each one had even achieved some minor celebrity status in New York City in those respective careers. M had also known someone during her high school years who had later become a famous singer/songwriter in the early 1970s, and I sometimes thought that M might feel better about herself if she could reconnect with this now famous person.

About a year into our new romance, we talked about taking the next step and moving in together. M had been living in Brooklyn, while I had been living on a farm near New Brunswick, New Jersey. We decided to try to find an apartment on Staten Island, in the area near the ferry to Manhattan. I didn't want to move back to Brooklyn at the time because I had found it much easier to play shows while living in New Jersey, not having to deal with the horrendous traffic problems that going in and out of Brooklyn usually meant. M would have preferred to stay in Brooklyn, but Staten Island seemed like a reasonable compromise at the time.

So we went hunting for an apartment in the St. George section of Staten Island. We found a place, and right around the beginning of September we moved in. We didn't have the place very well organized at first, with lots of stuff in boxes, but I figured that within a week or two we'd get it basically in order.

Then suddenly, a day or so after we had moved in together, M fell into a depression. I couldn't understand it. She spent days sitting in a chair staring out the window of the bedroom and other days when she didn't want to even get out of bed. I tried to help her maintain simple routines, like taking a shower and eating meals. Every morning, when she got out of the shower, she would be crying. I tried to get her to do a few simple tasks during the day, like taking a short walk, and sometimes she would, but other times it was just too much for her. She wouldn't do any painting, and I couldn't get her to read much of anything. I felt that if I hadn't been there, she might not have done anything at all.

What had caused this sudden bout of depression? I had no answer for that question. Of course I had to wonder if it had something to do with me and our new living situation. Of all the stuff that filled our little one bedroom apartment, at least three-fourths of it had been mine. Did the new living situation make her feel overwhelmed because the stuff in the apartment was so much more about me than her? Was there some other element in our situation of living together that put her into this state? I didn't think of myself as being such an overwhelming personality, but maybe I couldn't judge myself that clearly. Maybe living with me was more than she could handle.

We tried rearranging things in the apartment to help M feel more in control of her own area. I moved most of my stuff into the living room, and that became my space. The bedroom became M's area, with her paintings, her palette and her easel. However, this change didn't seem to have much of an effect.

What about the place itself? Could Staten Island be the cause of M's depression? She seemed to have some trouble trying to feel at home in the Staten Island neighborhood. I couldn't understand how the place could cause her problem, but in searching for a reason I felt that I had to consider every possibility. On Christmas day we went to her family's holiday gathering at her uncle's upper East Side apartment in Manhattan, and I talked extensively with M's parents about how she was feeling. M's parents both spoke about a time during M's childhood when they moved to Roosevelt, New Jersey, and how during this time M's mother had gone through an episode of depression. M's mother clearly had a very difficult time trying to adapt to life in Roosevelt, and could not manage to make the adjustment. After a while, the family found an apartment in Brooklyn, and once they got settled in there, M's mother felt fine.

The story of M's mother and Roosevelt told me that perhaps Staten Island could have something to do with M's problem. If M's mother could feel that disoriented by a place, maybe M could too. We talked about what we could possibly do in this case. Since M's parents still lived in Brooklyn, I thought maybe she could stay with them for a couple of weeks and see if that made her feel better. Her parents were willing to help out in whatever way that they could, so they agreed to let her move back in with them for a couple of weeks.

M's two week stay with her parents ended in one week. I came to visit her, and she begged me to take her back to Staten Island, which I did. She apparently felt even less at home returning to her parents' place, so that experiment ended abruptly.

I began to think about moving back to Brooklyn with M. Meanwhile, M's psychiatrist had changed her medication, concluding that for whatever reason the medication she had been using had stopped working. M also continued to see her therapist in Brooklyn once every week. I had no idea what, if anything, was working for her at that point, or what *would* work. I knew that episodes of depression had made her suicidal in the past, to the point where once she considered drinking a poison which would have surely killed her. I dreaded the thought that I would come home some time and find that she had taken her own life. I tried to do everything I could possibly think of to lift her spirits, but every morning she walked out of the shower in tears.

Then one night I returned to the apartment at a late hour, around one a.m., to find her wide awake and on a cleaning frenzy. "I'm back," she said with a smile. I hadn't seen her smile in such a long time, and it made me glad, but I didn't know what to make of all the sudden crazy energy, which seemed like a 180° turn from how she had been acting and feeling for months.

M's frantic energy level didn't last, as it turned out, and she would have a few more mornings with tears in the shower. However, as I found an apartment in Brooklyn, we made plans and began packing up for the move, in April of 1996, a short seven months after our Staten Island saga began, and her mood improved, so that by the time we settled into our place in Kensington, she had left both Staten Island and her depression behind.

So did Staten Island cause her depression? Not according to her psychiatrist. As we would learn over the next few months, M had been in the early stages of menopause, at such a young age that we had not guessed it could possibly be happening when her periods became irregular and then stopped completely. M's psychiatrist suggested that her depression medication had stopped working due to the major changes in her body chemistry, which had just begun to show up around the time we moved into the Staten Island apartment.

The body chemistry explanation from M's psychiatrist made sense, but the way in which her change in mood corresponded with the moves in and out of Staten Island still made it seem a bit spooky. The apartment we had lived in there sat at the top of a hill overlooking New York harbor, and the wind made ghostly sounds on the top of that hill that reminded me of something out of a Hitchcock soundtrack — I had never heard the wind make sounds like that in any of the many places I've lived or even visited over my entire life. I felt lucky that I had gotten M off of Staten Island and back to Brooklyn alive and in one piece.

On a side note, around this time, I remember starting to hear the phrase *Keith looks good*. After having avoided the spotlight for much of the previous two decades, Keith Richards had recently emerged and had begun making appearances on TV talk shows and such. People seemed to be falling all over each other saying, "Keith looks good." When I saw Keith in one of these appearances, I thought he looked like a man who had had a very hard life. I also thought that maybe doing heroin for twenty to thirty years isn't actually very good for a person. It occurred to me as well that maybe "Keith looks good" was really shorthand for "Keith is still alive — can you believe it?"

Along with the wonderful news about Keith, I read about Billy Corgan, the leader of Smashing Pumpkins, and how he said he had become a junkie out of his admiration for Keith, only to then realize how he had screwed himself up. As I read his tale, I asked myself what makes supposedly smart people act in such stupid ways. I had not wanted to believe the part that *monkey see monkey do* might play in the stories of heroin addiction, but here was one guy saying it so clearly I could hardly deny it.

Meanwhile back in Brooklyn, M and I would only be there for a couple of months before another major change would come our way, as I outline in the next chapter. I did not know what to make of the Staten Island experience, but I decided that we would think carefully before planning our next move. I had at least learned something about depression from the experience, though. I now understood that whatever set off the depression, once a person falls into that depression, they cannot simply walk it back. M spoke of it like falling into a deep well. Something happens to push you into the well, and once you're in it, you have no way to get yourself out. She told me, and I came to understand, that her condition was something that, by definition, the patient has no control over. If a person could stop feeling depressed through therapy or a change of furniture arrangements, then that person didn't have what M had. Psychiatrists and other mental health professionals use the term *Clinical Depression* to describe her condition.

At the end of that summer of 1996, I tried in vain to arrange a meeting between M and the famous singer/songwriter she had once known in that person's pre-fame era. I thought that connecting with this person might possibly help to brighten M's overall outlook, especially if the meeting went well, and I thought it probably would, given the reputation this particular singer/songwriter had for being a kind and generous soul. Through personal connections in the music business, I knew someone who played with the famous singer/songwriter's band, and when I heard from the music business grapevine about a special show in a special small place off the radar to be put on by the famous singer/songwriter and band, I asked my friend to get us tickets for this show. We got the tickets, and I also asked my friend about the possibility of arranging a meeting after the show between M and the famous person. My friend agreed to try to arrange that, but of course could make no guarantees. M and I went to the show, and really enjoyed a fine evening of singer/songwriter music, but when I spoke with my friend at the edge of the stage after the show, I was told that the famous performer had to leave the club as soon as the show ended. M and I left the little club that night a bit disappointed but not greatly surprised by the outcome. I continued to believe, at least for a while, that perhaps reconnecting on some level with people M had been close to in the past might help her overall mood in the present, though I seemed to have no luck with the effort.

Not long after, M would reunite with her three high school friends over the sad occasion of the death of one of their fathers. I had hoped that perhaps M could renew a friendship with one of the former quartet, but no such reconnection would happen. While I didn't completely give up on the idea after the funeral, I also saw how unlikely it was that M would be able to again be friends with anyone from her old high school circle. In my efforts to make M feel better about herself, I would get no help from her former high school friends or the famous singer/songwriter she once had known.

Chapter 13

Understanding Mom Because I Had To

Not long after M and I moved back to Brooklyn, in the spring of 1996, I began a creative collaboration with David Seitz, a Manhattan record producer who also had started his own record label a few years earlier. He originally called his record label Prime CD, and in later years it became Fifty Fifty Music. I had met David a few years earlier through my involvement with Fast Folk.

Jack Hardy and Richard Meyer had steered the Fast Folk creature through the early years of its existence. Jack's original vision had been about a monthly musical magazine, and he did his best to keep Fast Folk moving in that direction, although it didn't always come out on a monthly basis. Jack's vision had also included a performance space, and between the time I had left Fast Folk, in early 1993, and this time three years later, Jack had made that performance space a reality as well, but a short-lived reality that was about to end. Not surprisingly, making ends meet on even a small performance space in Manhattan proved to be too great a challenge for Jack's group of folkies.

With the lease on the Fast Folk Café about to expire, David called and asked me to help him save the Fast Folk LP and CD archives. All of Fast Folk's stock of LPs and CDs resided in the basement of the Fast Folk Café, and David proposed moving them from there to the Prime CD office, knowing that if they weren't moved they would be destroyed. Reluctantly, I agreed to help him do it. At that point I no longer had any great concern for Fast Folk, and I knew it would be a tedious and dirty task. As I headed over to the Fast Folk Café, I knew it would be a long night that I would not enjoy. It would turn out to be one of the worst nights of my life, and then it would get even worse when I got back to Brooklyn.

The basement of the Fast Folk Café was full of dust and dirt. After only a few loads up and down the stairs, we were sneezing, covered with dust. Once we loaded the cars, then we headed over to 26th Street and unloaded, carrying everything up the elevator to the fifth floor. Then we did it all over again. It was tiring, it was dirty, and it seemed endless. By the time we finished, the sun was coming up on Wednesday, July 3, the day before the beginning of the long holiday weekend.

I had hated it, but at least the task was done, and I headed back to Brooklyn. M and I had planned to spend the Fourth of July visiting my family upstate, and I didn't look forward to the four-hour drive after staying up all night, but I knew I'd have to do it. What I didn't know was the news that would hit me when I walked into my Brooklyn apartment. M was awake when I walked in, and she told me that my brothers had called a few times during the night to try to speak with me because our father had died.

What? How? How did this happen? What happened to him? My father had not been ill, he'd had no serious health problems, and he didn't exactly lead any sort of dangerous life style. How did he die? All I would learn in the next few days was that he came down with pneumonia, that he went into the hospital some time on Tuesday, and that he died later that night. Younger brother told me a couple of things that didn't quite add up, as well. He had visited our father at the hospital that night, and he said that Dad looked like he was in severe pain, and that some of his blood chemistry numbers were very strange.

At the funeral afterwards, when people asked me how he died, I had to tell them that we weren't really sure what happened. I won't elaborate on what I later came to understand, as it has no purpose in the context of this book, but I will say that he should not have died that night. His death would make the remaining years of my mother's life much harder for her and for those of us who cared for her.

So now my two brothers and I would have to focus on taking care of Mom. We had never had to truly understand her before, and though younger brother and I had been trying to piece it together over the previous few years, we now *had* to figure it out.

One of the first lessons I learned about Mom involved her medication. I had concluded that my grandmother, who had died five years earlier, probably would have lived longer if her heart medication hadn't caused her to lose her appetite for food. I resolved not to make the same mistake with Mom, so now that we were in charge of her, I wanted to track her medications and make sure that any problems got corrected.

One of the medications she took was specifically for her schizophrenia, and it had a few unpleasant side effects. It gave her a dry mouth, which made her want to drink a lot of fluids. It also gave her uncontrollable involuntary muscle movements, and it made it hard for her to control her bladder, so she would often wet herself. With all of these side effects, my mother told me she wanted to stop taking her schizophrenia medication. In my ignorance of her true situation and the possible consequences, I told her she could stop taking the schizophrenia medication, and she did.

I thought of all the questions I had about my mother's schizophrenia and the medications for it. Was this medication she was taking now really any kind of dramatic improvement over what she had taken thirty years earlier? I could guess that it probably was, but I didn't really know. I was certain that if I spoke with her psychiatrist, he would not want her to go off of her medication, but how much did he really understand her? I didn't know the answer to that question either.

What I really didn't know, though, was how typical this situation was. Schizophrenics often do what my mother was about to do. A schizophrenic will start taking a medication for the disease, and it will work against the symptoms of the disease, but also give the person truly unpleasant side effects, so the schizophrenic will stop taking the medication, and what happens? Very soon those symptoms return.

Not long after my mother stopped taking her medication, older brother caught her trying to open up all the doors and windows of the house, in the middle of a chilly February day, because she heard the voices of angels telling her to open up the house to the music of heaven. Older brother couldn't hear that heavenly music himself, but he could feel a distinct chill, and he started closing the doors and windows behind her. He soon had her back visiting her psychiatrist, and she was soon back on her schizophrenia medication.

I would have a number of conversations with Mom's psychiatrist over the next few years regarding the level of her medication. I learned that schizophrenia has an episodic nature, and sometimes it may come on strong, while at other times it might seem to recede into the background, and her medication would require adjustment accordingly.

So I had quickly learned that Mom's schizophrenia medication *did* work on some level in keeping her from hearing those voices in her head. It was a much different medication than the tranquilizer she and older brother had taken three decades earlier. It seemed much more effective, and that effectiveness seemed to be based on a much more complete understanding of the condition. I knew I didn't understand it, but I immediately had more respect for the psychiatrists who did.

In this period, I also learned that Mom had been an epileptic as a child, and had had a number of seizures during her younger years. The woman who had adopted her wanted to help her, but didn't have much knowledge about how to do so. She gave Mom ice baths in the hope of ending the seizures, and of course they had no effect. It made me feel sad to learn that this well-meaning woman who I had called my grandmother had caused such pain to my mother in her younger years.

At some point around this time I happened to catch a TV segment with an interview of Tom Cruise, and I found it quite troubling to hear Mr. Cruise say that psychiatry is not a genuine medical profession. He questioned the value of any psychiatric advice, and I soon learned that his views are the stated belief of the Church of Scientology to which he belongs. Listening to him, I wondered what he would do or say if he had a mother who opened the doors and windows of the house in the middle of winter because the voices in her head told her to let in the music of heaven.

Another TV segment I caught one night concerned modern methods of mapping brain activity. This show compared CAT scans of people with mental issues and people without mental issues. From this show I learned that schizophrenics seem to have a lower level of brain activity than people without mental issues, and that their brains make fewer connections.

Then one more TV segment finally opened up my understanding of Mom's mental condition. I watched a show about schizophrenics, which included a few stories of people with the disease. Somehow watching this show I finally understood what I never had before — that the voices in the schizophrenic's head were actual voices, not thoughts. Once my eyes opened to this, I felt foolish for never having understood before.

All at once, I could explain all of my mother's strange behavior for four decades. I understood immediately why she had done and said all of the weird things she had, and I saw how none of the family had ever come close to realizing this. Her disease was in reality not mystic or complicated.

Part of my newfound understanding came also from the realization that, as a psychiatrist had told me regarding M, psychiatric conditions usually have a psychological trigger. This fact often confuses the family of the patient, because the patient was fine before the trigger went off. In my mother's case, she was fine until the birth of her third child. She had given birth to two other children, but the third child caused her so much stress that it pushed her *over the edge*. Once over that edge, she could never return to the land of *the normal*.

The difference between psychiatric and psychological problems became clear to me in a way it had never been before. Our family saw my mother go through a very heavy psychological trauma with the birth of younger brother, but we did not clearly understand that this event triggered a psychiatric condition. Mom's genetic code had contained the possibility of this condition, but it took the psychological trigger to set it off. We the family saw her go through this psychological problem, but we never understood why, with time, she couldn't just get over it. She couldn't get over it because it wasn't about the psychological problem, it was about the psychiatric condition that resulted.

Psychiatrist use the term *broken brain* to refer to the nature of their patients' mental problems. All of a sudden I understood how aptly this term described my mother. Once Mom became a schizophrenic, she would forever be a schizophrenic — we do not yet know how to put the pieces of a broken brain back together.

Seeing Mom's broken brain clearly at last, I also saw how we, the members of her family who tried to care for her, had actually treated her badly at times without meaning to do so. Just as the older woman's use of ice baths could never have cured Mom's epilepsy, all of our attempts to affect her behavior and keep her from *going off the deep end* with threats and scoldings could never help heal her mind. The older man had often said, "It's all in the mind." He had never understood the broken brain any more than I did, and his saying implied that if Mom tried hard enough, she could have overcome her mental issues. No one expects the man with the broken arm to do pushups, simply because they can see the broken arm. No one can actually see the broken brain with an X-ray, though CAT scans and similar technologies are making the condition better understood. At any rate, Mom could never do those mental pushups with her broken brain, no matter what we her family expected of her.

Imagine hearing the voices that a schizophrenic does. From growing up with the adopted parents, my mother had very strong religious beliefs. She attended the Baptist Bible Seminary in Johnson City after high school, graduating, along with my father, in 1948. He had intended to become a preacher, and following graduation, the couple married and my father tried for a short time to make a living as a Baptist minister. Now imagine a few years later, when, after giving birth to my younger brother, Mom began having aural hallucinations. Hearing a voice coming out of nowhere, Mom, given her religious background, would surely have believed that she was hearing the voice of God or an angel. She would also likely not have questioned whatever crazy things such a voice told her to do as long as she believed that she was hearing God or an angel.

In my own experiences with schizophrenia, I have noticed that the voices in the schizophrenic's head don't ever seem to tell the person to do good things. I've never known of a schizophrenic who heard a voice telling him or her to compliment someone or do something nice for someone. Almost universally, in everything I've read or heard, the voices tell the schizophrenic to do something that will harm either someone else and/or the schizophrenic himself/herself. I would guess that psychiatrists know more about the specifics of this than I do, but I can see that the voices the schizophrenic hears come from the darker *devil's advocate* regions of the brain. When I tried to suggest to my mother, during a later episode, that perhaps the voices she heard come not from God or heaven's angels but maybe from angels from the darker side, my mother refused to even allow *that* possibility.

So for much of my mother's life, she had episodes where she heard voices. She probably usually believed that God or angels were telling her something, but her family and her psychiatrist were telling her a different story. Now if God or the angels told you something, but your family and your doctor told you something else, who would you believe? Would she risk angering God or the angels if she didn't listen to them? My mother lived with these questions for most of her adult life. During this time, the family members who tried to care for her sometimes, without intending to do so, treated her meanly and coldly. Finally, younger brother and I came to understand her only because we had to become more directly involved in her care, due to her husband's death.

Older brother may not have ever understood Mom, though living with her as a daily basis, he saw more closely the effects of it. Having finally understood the nature of her disease, and the role of a psychological trigger in setting it off, I came to the conclusion that older brother probably carried the genetic code for the disease just as our mother had, but he had no psychological trauma to set it off. During his late teens and his entire twenties, he continued to live with the parents and grandparents, and they treated him like a big child. They bought him clothes, made him meals, gave him a roof over his head without charging him rent, and so on. He lived a very calm life, not having to ever worry about his next meal or how to pay his rent. I had wondered, during this time, if he might have developed a bit more maturity if he had had to pay rent somewhere and make his own meals, but with a more complete understanding of schizophrenia a few decades later, I decided that it was a lucky thing for the family that older brother had lived such a calm life. Having one more member in our circle hearing voices would have made our existence as a family much more difficult, and so looking back, I can be thankful that older brother lived the way he did during the time when the disease might have severely affected him as well.

Chapter 14

The Sock Drawer Moment

Looking back, it seems hard to believe that, having made the mistake of letting Mom stop taking her mental medication, I would turn around and let the same thing happen with M. The inevitable result would not come as soon with M as it had with Mom, but it would also take a lot longer to undo the mistake, though in the process, I would finally see her condition clearly.

Not long after moving back to Brooklyn in the spring of 1996, M had learned that someone she had known in high school was now taking lithium, and probably would have to do so for the rest of her life. M and I then spoke about how sad it was for someone to have to rely on a drug for the rest of their life, and in that context, we both thought about M's own situation and how that might play out in the future. Little did we know then where such conversation and such ideas would lead us in a few short years.

M told me she was a *finder*, and she proved this to me many times by finding items I misplaced in various odd corners of our apartment. Then, in the fall of 1997, having been back in Brooklyn for a year and a half, she found something I didn't even know existed — she found us a better, bigger and nicer apartment for slightly less rent than what we had been paying.

The new place had a large room at both ends, with a hallway connecting them. On one side of the hallway was the kitchen and a small bedroom, while the other side of the hallway held the bathroom and entrance. The kitchen was small, but still big enough to comfortably hold a table for two by the window. The kitchen window had a beautiful view of the back yard of the house next door, and a huge tree standing in that back yard. Yes, a tree was growing in Brooklyn — in this case big, beautiful and very green in the warm weather months. On a sunny day, the kitchen and the small bedroom next to it had so much sunlight it could lift a person's spirits a couple of notches just walking into one of them.

Naturally, the small bedroom became M's studio, being the perfect room for an artist who wanted to make use of natural light. M and I finally had a living space that suited her artistic needs, and we both felt really pleased with this very special *find* of hers. I also liked living in Borough Park better than Kensington, at least in part because the struggle to find a parking place on the alternate side *night befores* usually only involved no more than a five to ten minute search, as opposed to the half-hour to full hour that search had taken in Kensington.

When we moved in, we loved the place, but we could not have imagined how much it possibly could, and would, change in just a few short years. The house next door had been vacant, with a *For Sale* sign out in front, but we did not have any idea what would happen when that sign came down.

Having found a really nice place in Brooklyn that we both liked, I no longer had any concerns about the Staten Island curse. Now having passed through the changes of menopause, M would more than likely never again go through any great changes in her body chemistry. M talked with me about the unpleasant side effects of her medication, which included a dry mouth and constipation. Probably the most unpleasant side effect, though, is how distance it makes a person feel from their own feelings. Creative people of every type use their feelings to fuel their creative efforts, and the distance created by the medication makes it harder to get in touch with those feelings. M also wondered, as did I, whether or not it was necessary to continue with the medication. As the Staten Island crisis faded into the past, so did our sense of concern about that crisis. We were learning that psychiatric conditions are often episodic, and so we reasoned that if M was not in an episode of depression, perhaps she didn't need to continue taking her medication. Some time in the late spring or early summer of 2000, during our third year in our wonderful top-floor sunlit Borough Park apartment, M decided, after several conversations with her therapist and her psychiatrist, to stop taking her depression medication. The two of them didn't favor this decision, and they warned us of possible serious consequences, but they didn't prevent M from doing what she wanted to do.

At first, M felt happy to be free of the medication, and its unpleasant side effects. She had told me long before this about how, during her first really dark episode of depression years before I met her, when she learned of the existence of medication that could treat her condition, she had insisted to her therapist and others that she be given such medication. Now, if possible, she wanted nothing more to do with it.

Meanwhile, our little Borough Park apartment world was about to undergo major change. The *For Sale* sign had come down from the house next door, and what the landlady told us about the plans for that lot did not sound good. The new owner planned to put up a building slightly taller than our house and built right to the property line, only two feet away from our windows. We didn't like what we were hearing about the new plans, though M and I figured that we would simply have to adjust to whatever happened if and when it did.

One day during the warm months of 2001, the excavator arrived next door and tore down the house. Some of what that machine did caused our house to shake, and in so doing made us both a bit edgy. The big, beautiful tree in the back yard next door came down, and did we miss that! The piles of materials arrived, and soon after the groups of workmen.

M, who had already gone for well over a year without her depression medication, began to feel troubled. As she tried to paint or draw in her sunny studio room, she felt the workmen watching her and making fun of her. I couldn't really say if they were doing this or not, but I did feel that they acted like a bunch of goons, and I didn't enjoy having them around for the 12 to 14 hours per day that they were there, sometimes even on the weekends.

As the story of the building next door unfolded, other bad events, great and small, piled on. During a heavy thunderstorm in mid-August, our heat came on strongly, and I couldn't shut it off. The apartment got unbearably hot, I couldn't run the air conditioners due to problems with the electrical circuits, and I couldn't open the windows because of the heavy downpour outside. I began having a series of painful and expensive tooth problems, as I have had at various different points in my life. A very dark political situation seemed to be taking shape on the big stage, with the 9/11 attacks, the anthrax attacks that followed a month later and then the Draconian measures of the Patriot Act, all pointing towards the violence, war and bad economics that would unfold over the next few years.

While I tried to remain optimistic in the face of a lot of trouble in that fall of 2001, the workmen next door got the building higher and higher until it got to our level, and then we had the wonderful experience of having them even closer than they had been before. One Sunday morning, as we shared a meal at our kitchen table, a pair of them startled us by walking by within a few feet of us just outside of our window. Being on our level took their intrusions into our lives to a whole new level as well. We no longer felt as if we had any privacy whatsoever in our apartment. We felt as if a group of goons was constantly watching us, and that they even knew when we used the bathroom.

Of course, we also knew it would end eventually. They had a job to do, and we knew that soon they would be putting up a wall that would from then on keep the sunlight from reaching our kitchen window, and M's studio window as well. A day or two before we expected that wall to go up, we had a personal tragedy unfold as we lost a pet that was near and dear to us both. It was in the midst of this sadness, losing a favorite pet, that M told me she was falling apart. I felt truly sad losing our pet, and I had probably been more attached to the animal than M, but I tried to tell her not to get too carried away by the sadness. We already knew the shared pain of losing a pet we loved, and we would surely experience it again, but it wasn't and shouldn't be on the same level as, say, losing a parent. I told her then, even at the heart of the loss, that she needed to keep a perspective on that loss. She told me that I didn't understand, and that it wasn't that much about the loss of the pet — it was about the loss of her own emotional footing, and this had been happening for a few days. Once again, she was feeling the way she had on Staten Island.

This conversation happened on a night shortly before Thanksgiving. M and I had planned, as usual, to visit my family upstate for the holiday weekend, and on the day before Thanksgiving, we loaded the car and left the apartment. As we did so, the workmen next door were putting up the brick wall that would block out our sunlight. When I got up that Wednesday morning, on a bright and sunny day, the sunlight was still streaming in through the kitchen window, over the top of the wall more than halfway constructed, and I thought that maybe there was a possibility that some direct sunlight might still reach that window when they finished the job. When we returned at the end of the long holiday weekend, I knew *that* would never happen. Our apartment which had once had such beautiful views of the tree and back yard next door, and which had a kitchen that glowed on bright and sunny mornings, had now become a cave. From much of the apartment, you could now no longer tell the difference between a bright and sunny morning and a heavily overcast dark grey afternoon. And as dark as our sunny apartment had now become, so too had our lives now become, as M slid into her second major episode of depression since we had gotten together.

With M now in the grip of a new episode of depression, her psychiatrist restarted her mental medication, with all of us agreeing that it was the necessary thing to do. I got used to helping M once again with most of the details of her life, which include helping her decide what to wear every day. I had learned, or at least partly understood from her previous episode, as she had repeated to me many times, that the feeling of clinical depression is not one of sadness, but one of being overwhelmed by the simplest and smallest decisions of life, ones that *normal* people take for granted because they have no trouble doing them. I also clearly understood that she had no control over this feeling.

Then one morning, as we tried to figure out what socks M would wear that day, the whole picture became clear to me, almost in a single moment. In the midst of the sock decision, she looked at me tearfully and said, "What is there left to live for?" I had heard those words, spoken in that same tone of voice, from a tape of Kurt Cobain almost eight years before, but when I heard her say it, I immediately remembered him. Now someone was standing next to me, saying the same thing, and feeling the same thing, but this time it was somebody I cared for very much and who I really wanted and needed to understand. Suddenly, I did understand.

The first thing I saw very clearly was that the feeling inside the person's head has no connection with that person's objective reality. M had a drawer full of clean socks, and practically any pair would be fine — the decision about which pair of socks to wear was a small and inconsequential one.

At the moment when Kurt said, from his hospital bed, "What is there left to live for?" he had no connection with the real circumstances of his life. He had a beautiful and caring wife, a lovely newborn daughter and a fabulously successful rock-and-roll career, but from inside of his head, he could not make any connection with *any* of that reality. All he could feel, at that moment, was his own inability to make even the smallest and most inconsequential decision.

Where does this lack of confidence come from? Why does a person in a deep depression make mountains out of mole hills, and then feel unable to climb them? As I had heard the TV commercials say, it is due to an imbalance of naturally-occurring chemicals in the brain. When I first heard this phrase, it sounded to me like typical Madison Avenue *adspeak*. After all, I had over the years seen many people give themselves an imbalance in caffeine in their brains, for the purpose of helping them stay awake. However, I finally saw clearly just how deep this chemical imbalance runs for those with major depression, or those at the depression end of bipolar disorder. I also realized at that moment with M and the sock drawer that if I had such a chemical imbalance in my brain as she did at that moment, I would also not know how to figure out which socks to wear.

Suddenly, I didn't feel so superior to all of those junkie musicians. Instead, I simply felt lucky I had dodged the genetic bullet that took down all of them, as well as the schizophrenic one that took down my mother and my mother's mother. I didn't have any of these problems because I didn't have the genetic code that caused them. I was not a better or smarter person, or one with a stronger character than these people — I simply didn't have what they had.

The sock drawer moment also made me realize how simple this condition actually is. I had looked for reasons and causes in M's life, and had wanted to make her feel better about herself. I had hoped to help her reconnect with at least one person she had been closer to in her younger years, thinking that this might help to lighten her mood. I now realized that none of that would have changed a thing. When that chemical imbalance arrives, and the person falls into that deep well, the only way out is to restore the chemical balance somehow. The experience of the wall going up next door, and the invasions of our privacy in our own apartment, had presented the psychological trigger that had pushed M into the well, but also the chemical imbalance had occurred because she had stopped taking her mental medication. That chemical imbalance had crept up on her slowly, and now she would slowly have to restore it by taking that medication again. It would take many months, and for much of that time, M would say through tears that she didn't believe the medication was actually working. In fact, it took so long to work that we spoke with her psychiatrist about beginning a different medication, which would have meant starting the process from scratch, and we decided to give the old medication one more week before making the switch. Fortunately, in that week, the chemical balance finally returned, and M could smile again. She emerged from the depression, and we resolved to never try any more experiments with her medication. We both felt thankful for the existence of such medications, and for the understanding of the chemical imbalances at the root of major depression. That understanding comes, at least in part, from the psychiatrists and psychologists who work with people suffering from mental problems, and my respect for the members of these professions has grown as my own understanding of these conditions has grown. At points along the way, a simple answer from M's psychiatrist, her psychologist, or my mother's psychiatrist, helped to light the way to that greater understanding.

Chapter 15

What Can I Tell You?

What can I tell you? What did I learn about depression (and by extension, the depression end of bipolar disorder) from M? What did I learn about schizophrenia from my mother? First and foremost, a person with one of these conditions has a broken brain. Each one of these conditions happens due to a physical problem in the brain.

Also, someone with a broken arm has the advantage over someone with a broken brain. First, people can see a broken arm but cannot see a broken brain. Second, a broken arm, if treated properly, can heal itself, whereas a broken brain cannot. Schizophrenia, clinical depression and bipolar disorder are lifetime sentences. Once a person falls prey to one of these psychiatric disorders, that person will never be free of the condition. Western medicine, at this point in the second decade of the 21st century, has no cure for any of these conditions, and can only treat the symptoms, not the root causes.

However, these conditions are also episodic in nature, so it can be possible for someone with one of these psychiatric problems to temporarily believe that the disease has somehow been cured, when that person is in the breathing space between episodes. That breathing space can even be a year or longer, as it was in M's case, before the condition reappears, but in most if not all cases it will reappear. With the infinite variety of human experience, it might be possible to find exceptions to this rule, but if they do exist, I would expect them to be extremely rare.

Here I want to draw a clear line between psychology and psychiatry. I would liken a person with psychological issues to someone trapped in a sort of mental maze — if a person caught in such a maze takes the right steps, that person might eventually find the way out of the maze. I would liken a person with a psychiatric condition to someone who falls into a well — no matter how that person retraces steps, there is no way to step back and get out of the well.

Therein lies some of the confusion surrounding these conditions. These psychiatric problems almost always have a psychological trigger that sets them off, and people often seem to confuse the cause with the result. In my family's case, the psychological trauma around my younger brother's birth pushed my mother over the edge into schizophrenia. We her family did not clearly understand that following that event my mother had become someone completely different from her former self — she was now a schizophrenic, and would continue to be one for the rest of her life, even though she might have extended periods when she did not hear voices in her head. She did not simply have a deep psychological wound or scar, she was completely changed. No amount of attention to her psychological issues would ever change her back. She could visit old friends for a couple of weeks in a very relaxed setting far away from the site of her deep emotional trauma, with as little around her to remind her of the troubles as possible, but no amount of relaxation, good times or good feelings would take her back to the place where she wasn't a schizophrenic. Had she lived a very placid and pleasant existence for the rest of her life, which of course wasn't possible, she still could not have found her old self.

We her family thought that much of Mom's problems came from her basic living situation. My father never made enough money to provide for his family, so I grew up in the house of the couple who had adopted Mom as a child, and the conflicts this caused were many and varied. I can remember plenty of loud and bitter arguments. At the time it seemed reasonable to conclude that Mom would have fared much better mentally without those issues, but the reality that I now see so clearly is that the living situation only made a bad condition worse. Even if my father had had a good-paying job and we could have lived in a nice, modern place with just the parents and the three boys, it would not have cured Mom's schizophrenia. A person deep into an episode of one of these psychiatric conditions has little connection with the reality of their own life, so while a bad living situation can make things worse, an ideal situation can provide little or no relief from the problems.

In the case of people with clinical depression, or those on the depression end of bipolar disorder, the tears they cry are not from sadness but from despair. People often make the mistake of looking for some sort of epic sadness in the lives of those who experience these forms of depression as a way to explain why these people feel the way they do. What someone in that dark state *really* feels is a sense of being overwhelmed by the simplest of tasks. M could not decide, at the sock drawer moment, what pair of socks to wear that day. A person in this state feels extreme confusion at all waking moments, and a total inability to make even the smallest and most insignificant decision. A person with balanced brain chemistry knows how little the socks matter, but the person in this depressed state *doesn't* know that. M told me that she has no physical pain associated with this state, and as far as I know this is generally true of people in this kind of depression, but the psychic anguish of this feeling is enough to drive someone to commit suicide, as Kurt Cobain did and as M came close to doing.

While I have used the analogy of a broken arm in places to illustrate the physical nature of psychiatric problems, it might be more useful at times to picture an amputated arm. A person who develops schizophrenia, depression or bipolar disorder has truly lost a part of their brain. Part of the time they might be able to function just fine, just as a one-armed person can still read, converse and do many of the other regular tasks of living, but at some point the lack of the missing part can and will cause them big problems.

So why does someone end up with a broken brain? The answer lies in genetics. People in my family would often remark on how well my mother's sister had done in life. She married a man who became an electrician, and the couple raised eight children together. From all indications, they had a pretty good life together, and had none of the problems of our household. Around the edges of these facts seemed to lurk the implication that something was lacking in my mother's character. Somehow she was the *bad* girl, the one who picked the wrong man to marry, and the one who caused all of the problems. What actually made her the trouble child was the fact that she carried the same genetic predisposition to schizophrenia as her mother. Mom's real mother, that crazy woman who had lived in a shack near Freeville with all her dogs and cats and no indoor plumbing, had a brother who was not schizophrenic, and who had a very successful career as a golf celebrity in our area, but we never met him, apparently because he wanted nothing to do with his *crazy* sister and any of her children. Mom had both an older sister and a younger brother, and neither of them were schizophrenic. Mom had three boys, and my younger brother and I had no issues with schizophrenia. My older brother never had a moment when he started hearing voices, probably because he lived a very placid existence during the time when he would have been vulnerable to that aspect of the disease. Older brother did have many of the low level symptoms of the disease, however, and while I never spoke with the psychiatrist who looked after him in his younger years, it wouldn't surprise me now if I were to learn that he was officially diagnosed as a schizophrenic during the time he was under the man's care.

So it goes with genetics. Maybe one child has good teeth (older brother) and the other children have bad teeth (younger brother and I). So also one child carries the genetic code for the possibility of schizophrenia (my mother) and the other children don't (her older sister and younger brother). Genetics determine a lot of the physical and mental issues of humanity, from susceptibility to diseases like cancer to our sensitivity to hot and cold temperatures, and each one of us carries a unique code. The fact that my mother carried the genetic possibility for schizophrenia did not make her better or worse than her brother and sister who didn't carry that code. Understanding the genetic root of schizophrenia has also led me to wonder about my grandmother's parents and earlier generations.

Having reached a basic understanding of schizophrenia, depression and bipolar disorder, I can now clearly see how these conditions explain many aspects of human behavior. During the time I grew up, in the 1960s, I remember various discussions about alcoholism. Growing up in a household of very religious people who didn't touch alcohol, we looked upon all forms of alcohol consumption as some sign of weakness of character or lack of will power. One element of the discussion about alcoholism centered on the repetition of the addiction across multiple generations. Did the children of alcoholics learn the behavior as children and simply do as adults what their parents had done, or was there a genetic element to the story?

Then something began to happen in the 1960s, and continued to happen in the 1970s — the children of alcoholics became drug addicts, largely moving to the hard drugs of heroin and cocaine. One could explain this at the time by simply saying that drugs had become, for the 1960s generation, what alcohol had been for previous generations, and truly drugs became more commonplace and had greater acceptance than they had had before.

In recently reading the biography of a famous musician of the time, I learned that this person's family had a long history of alcoholism. The musician's father had build a highly-successful professional career for himself, only to then turn around and nearly destroy that career with bouts of alcoholism. For much of my life I had read similar stories, had wondered why someone would do this and had never gotten an answer that made sense. I knew that this musician had had episodes of deep depression, but I also read about periods of unbelievable high energy which included an incident of jumping on top of a friend's car while it was moving. The book I read belongs to a good friend who works as a doctor, treating people with substance abuse and addiction problems. When I remarked to him that I had concluded that a large percentage of people with addiction and substance abuse issues are self-medicating for psychiatric and psychological issues, of which many are probably undiagnosed, he reacted as if I'd just mentioned that two plus two equals four. In his line of work, such an assertion is an obvious statement of fact that he has seen in his practice too many times to even begin to count.

Understanding the nature of bipolar disorder explains this whole story that played out publicly in so many rock-and-roll careers in the 1960s and 1970s, and privately in many other lives. Someone at the top end of the bipolar cycle has highly-elevated levels of the brain chemicals that are lacking on the depression end, and in that top state, they can and will take on any task with an energy that seems almost super-human. On the top end, many bipolar people create highly successful careers for themselves. Then when the low point comes, as it usually does, and the bipolar person can hardly get out of bed, no one around him or her can understand what happened to all that super-human energy. Friends look for explanations but can find nothing to answer the question.

Some time over the last few years, I heard an interview with David Crosby, and in it he mentioned that his (our) generation had been right about many things, including Viet Nam, but they (we) were wrong about drugs. Earlier in my life I would have agreed with him, but now I don't. When a chemical imbalance in the brain lies at the root cause of someone's problem, then it makes sense to try to restore the chemical balance. Another famous musician, who is known to have had a heroin problem in the 1960s and 1970s, said in a recent interview, "I didn't take heroin to feel good, I took heroin to feel normal." Heroin can sometimes mimic the action of the missing brain chemicals much better than alcohol, so it can work better as a substitute self-medication. A person in a state of clinical depression, or in the depression end of bipolar disorder, may possibly temporarily restore their ability to function normally, and at least figure out what socks to wear, by taking heroin. I want to be clear about this point, not to advocate for heroin use but to give people a better understanding of why this drug has become so much more widespread in our society, in the hope that eventually, with greater understanding, we as a nation and as a society will evolve a better public policy regarding this issue.

There are, of course, a number of legally-prescribed drugs that also address the chemical imbalance that causes unipolar depression, and thankfully, M has been pulled out of the abyss by them a few times. The drugs do have unpleasant side effects, though, and the most significant of these for a creative artist can be the degree to which they distance the taker from emotion. Much of creativity relies on the feelings an artist can express, whether playing guitar, writing, moving paint across a canvas or whatever. I have no doubt, in looking back, that Kurt Cobain was bipolar, and I take his song *Lithium* as a clue that he tried that for a while to address his problems. I would guess that maybe before he did that he self-medicated with heroin, and I think he made the conscious decision to go back to self-medicating with heroin because he found it difficult to be creative while on lithium. Heroin use has its own perils under our current system that criminalizes it, but for a bipolar person this route has addition risks, including the possibility of feeling so bad that the sufferer might commit suicide, which is what Kurt did. Realizing that he probably knew the risks and decided to forego the lithium anyway, all for the sake of his creativity, makes me feel a lot more for him years later than I ever did at the time that it all went down. I also can understand why an artist might not want to take these risks, and I can respect the decision either way. I also feel lucky that I myself never had to make such a decision.

One other point to understand about schizophrenia and major depression is that they are not mystic and complex creatures, and once you see them for what they are, they are nearly as mundane as a broken arm. No one waxes poetic about a broken arm, and a broken brain is nothing to write poetry about either. You could be a perfectly happy person who's never been touched by mental issues, but if someone could come along, stick a straw into your head and suck the appropriate brain chemicals out of your head down to the level of someone with major depression, you would find yourself in bed crying, "What is there left to live for?"

Schizophrenia can be a bit trickier to decipher, in that only the person who hears the voices knows what those voices are saying, but once the observer clearly understands that they're watching someone who's having aural hallucinations, that observer basically has a handle on the situation. While my mother, to the best of my knowledge, rarely if ever had visual hallucinations, I learned from the movie *A Beautiful Mind* that some schizophrenics do, but whether aural or visual or both, the hallucinations all come from inside the person's mind, and not from some door into another dimension or some supernatural deity. That said, I think it's likely that, up to a certain point in my own life, if I heard a voice speaking to me and seeming to come out of nowhere, I would also probably have thought it was the voice of God or an angel.

Understanding this now, I see why my mother would be snapping her fingers by her ears on that night we went to the State Hospital — she wanted to stop the sound of those voices. I also understand her wearing headphones, much later in life — again, she wanted to hear something other than those voices.

The final related lesson I can share is one I've had to relearn over and over again in my life: "Judge not, lest ye be judged." I learned that Bible verse at a very young age, but I have had to relearn its true meaning a number of times throughout the years. No one can know the pain that someone else feels, so no one should judge someone else too harshly for doing what they need to do to relieve their suffering. The pain someone feels in a state of unipolar depression is not physical but purely psychic, but that suffering is extreme enough to drive many of them to suicide. I don't know the pain of major depression, but I do now understand, have seen M go through a number of episodes of this experience, that I can and should be grateful that I've never experienced that pain. I think we need to show our fellow travelers in this life as much understanding and compassion as we can, and to try to help those who truly need our help, as these people do. We do not do ourselves or our society any good by criminalizing their behavior and punishing them for what they feel they need to do.

Of course, schizophrenia presents a number of difficult questions, and I don't claim to have the answers for all of them. I'm grateful that the type of schizophrenia running through my family's genetics is *disorganized schizophrenia* because I recognize the fact that paranoid schizophrenics often act in violent and uncontrollable ways. A paranoid schizophrenic may try to kill someone because the voices in his head tell him that this person is trying to kill him. The obvious answer to this dilemma is to keep all paranoid schizophrenics in institutions where they can be closely watched. However, modern medications make it possible for paranoid schizophrenics to live relatively normal lives, so keeping them all institutionalized could seem cruel and unnecessary. Yet, what often happens is that the paranoid schizophrenic, while trying to live a relatively normal existence, comes to believe that he or she is feeling fine and doesn't need to continue taking the schizophrenic medication, which also

My mother and her own real mother, sometime in the 1990s. My mother's real mother would die in 2001, at the age of 98.

always has unpleasant side effects, so he or she stops taking the medication, and then not long after lashes out in some violent way when the voices return. I don't really have an answer to this vexing dilemma, but I do think it warrants better understanding and serious discussion. Hopefully, from that understanding and discussion will come better ideas and suggestions than what I can personally offer at this time.

So I hope my personal journey has been of some use to the reader. I don't claim to have complete knowledge of schizophrenia or depression, and I continue to learn, so my journey continues, but I have come to clearly understand a few basic points about schizophrenia and depression that I feel the public at large continues to misunderstand. I hope this book can play a part in expanding the dialog around psychiatric and psychological conditions, and clear up some of this misunderstanding.

One More Broken Thing

Has anyone here seen my old friend?
He used to play guitar.
He had the style, he had the heart.
He could have been better than most of them
but he never made the stars.

Someone said they might have seen
someone who might have been him
stumbling in a haze again,
looking kind of beat on a dead-end street
down near where the junk man is.

The junk man, he will sell you things —
things you don't need to buy —
a broken doll that always cries,
a clock with broken springs,
a bird with broken wings,
a broken pair of dice.

And so I guess my friend is gone
and I'm remembering
a song I once heard him sing
but if I have the song
all the junk man's got is one more broken thing.

© 1988, 2012 Twice Told Tunes

(from my 2012 CD release *Who Said What*, which is a remix
version of a 1988 cassette-only release)

Ship in a Bottle

He sails a ship in a bottle of whiskey.
He takes to drinking and it takes him to sea.
He finds no message in his bottle uncorked
but he sways with the tide all down the block.

He captains a flying dutchman,
he just can't bring her home.
Can you spare a little something
to help him keep afloat?

He sees a girl on a stormy shore alone
combing her hair with a fish bone,
diamonds flashing on the tops of the waves.
He calls but she can't hear what he says.

He captains a flying dutchman...

He kills his bottle in the spot where he lays
and buries it with a crash in the alleyway.
Cobwebs at the corners of his eyes
are the nets and rigging this sailor's known by.

He captains a flying dutchman...

© 1991, 2009 Twice Told Tunes

(from my 2009 CD release *Elder Street*)